A REPORT ON GOVERNMENT PROCUREMENT PRACTICES

A REPORT ON GOVERNMENT PROCUREMENT PRACTICES

Stanley Fishner

CAMELOT PUBLISHERS
P.O. BOX 2910
MERRIFIELD, VIRGINIA 22116-2910

ISBN 0-9606848-2-4
Library of Congress Catalog Card Number 87-092078

Contents

ABBREVIATIONS

ACO	Administrative Contracting Officer
B&P	bid and proposal (expense)
CAP	contractor-acquired property
CASB	Cost Accounting Standards Board
CBD	*Commerce Business Daily*
CFR	Code of Federal Regulations
CGS	cost of goods sold
CICA	Competition in Contracting Act
CO	Contracting Officer
CPFF	cost plus fixed fee (contract)
CS	Contract Specialist (buyer)
DCAA	Defense Contract Audit Agency
DCASMA	Defense Contract Administration Services Management Area
DCASMARO	Defense Contract Administration Services Management Area Regional Office
D/L	direct labor
DLA	Defense Logistics Agency
DOD	Department of Defense
FAR	Federal Acquisition Regulation
FFP	firm fixed price (contract)
FPI	fixed price incentive (contract)
G&A	general and administrative (expense)
GAAP	generally accepted accounting practices
GFE	government-furnished equipment
GFP	government-furnished property
IFB	Invitation for Bid; sealed bid; full and open competition
IG	Inspector General
IND/L	indirect labor
IR&D	independent research and development
OFPP	Office of Federal Procurement Policy
O.H.	overhead, manufacturing overhead, burden, or factory expense

OIG . . . . Office of the Inspector General
OMB . . . . Office of Management and Budget
P&L . . . . profit and loss—or income (statement)
PCO . . . . Procurement Contracting Officer
PR . . . . procurement request
RFP . . . . Request for Proposal; competitive,
negotiated; full and open competition
RFQ . . . . Request for Quotation; sole source,
negotiated; other than full and open
competition
S.E. . . . . selling expense
SEB . . . . source evaluation board
T&M . . . . time and material (contract)
TCO . . . . Termination Contracting Officer

Introduction

This nation needs the most formidable military capability in the world. Yet people in and out of the government are trading on the need in a wholesale exploitation of the present governmental procurement process. The country's economic foundation therefore becomes sabotaged, while the needed military capability continues to deteriorate. Countless commissions issue innumerable reports on the government's acquisition process, yet the basic problems remain unaddressed. Sensitive, critical issues lack appeal as targets for reform, especially when potential reforms would strip major industries of "bread and butter" subsidies and require honest accountings. Hence, recommended "actions" have promoted the very foxes to guard the chicken coop they stalk, and in the existing political climate the process perpetuates itself. No amount of money appropriated for "defense" will ever be sufficient to give this nation its needed defense. The entire acquisition process has been stalemated by legislation that clones cost overruns and rewards inefficiency.

To label the process "flawed" is to grossly understate the gravity of the situation. Many would blame industry alone for overruns and excessive prices, yet the government has established the rules and industry has been left to play within those confines. Accordingly, to effect any meaningful change, the rules must first be altered. Similarly, the attitudes of legislators and agency personnel toward contractors must also change.

The all-encompassing acquisition process covers initiation of requirements, engineering, logistics, budgeting, appropriations, maintenance, repair, and procurement. Procurement (which includes the treatment of costs for government contracts) is only one function in the overall process; nevertheless, it is the single function most ignored in commission reports dealing with the subject and the one requiring the greatest changes.

Problems in procurement remain governmentwide, yet four very disturbing patterns have evolved: (1) the deterioration of the industrial base accompanied by a significant decrease in the dollar value of prime government contracts awarded to small businesses; (2) an unprecedented concentration of prime government procurement dollars (approximately 90% or $177 billion of the government's total 1987 procurement expenditures) in a small number of firms (approximately 200); (3) erosion of the nation's technological superiority; and (4) a significant increase in subsidies to large businesses. Logically, government procurement practices ought to be comparable to those employed in the private sector, and the government should treat its suppliers the same way major corporations treat their suppliers for nongovernment goods and services: the audit of major suppliers' accounting records; closer scrutiny of production and human resources; and the use of flexible costing and pricing practices. Special considerations granted to giant corporations should be eliminated—or greatly curtailed: Present forms of subsidies have no place if the nation is to repair its deteriorated industrial base.

Reform requires an analysis of the impact of government procurement on our economy and of the government's role in using the procurement process as an instrument for achieving national, social, and economic objectives. The "political-military-industrial" complex has stifled meaningful changes in the process, and it is a force that must be dealt with. President Eisenhower coined the phrase "military-industrial complex" which today has to include congress—the political aspect of the process.

Conservatively estimated, the government could procure approximately 20% (an astronomical $40 billion) more hardware and services annually, within its present programmed procurement budget, simply by changing the manner in which government contractors treat costs. Another 5-10% could be gained by changing elementary procurement procedures and practices. Similarly, other improvements could effect more accurate programming, planning, and budgeting to limit or control cost growth. The obvious implications are prodigious.

The changes required to effect these savings are neither earthshaking nor revolutionary; however, they would be impossible to implement under the present system in which government procurement is neither run nor operated by procurement personnel. Instead, heads of departments, administrators, project personnel, and policy personnel dictate to procurement personnel (a group considered a "service organization") what they will buy and how they will buy it. Simply put, too many quarterbacks outside the procurement offices have too little experience in buying goods for the government and too little knowledge of statutes and regulations. Time-honored consideration of economy, budgeting, and legality are nonexistent; rather, the practice today entails adoption and creation of new laws and regulations to reflect the manner in which the job was in fact accomplished. This situation remains the "norm," particularly at the Defense Contract Audit Agency (DCAA), the agency responsible for the majority of cost audits of government contractors, where most audits lack any meaningful information to assist a buyer in a negotiation. The true condition of a contractor's accounting system remains obfuscated in the audit reports.

These condititions did not just happen; they have been brewing since the late 1950s. Abuses have been known but ignored or whistle-blowers and boat rockers summarily dismissed. The situation is worse governmentwide, where the Office of the Inspector General (comprised of former DCAA auditors who were pioneers in the loose interpretation and implementation of regulations) has been given more authority.

The present political environment fosters the procurement crisis through job security, awards, and promotions. Checks and balances remain illusory and fanciful.

The result has been a significant increase in cost growth and cost overruns during the past 25 years. Treatises have stressed the monetary side of cost overruns and cost growth in defense contracts, generally criticizing the services' monitoring of defense programs and playing up the military-industrial complex. Specific firms and contracts have been indicted. But incomplete and distorted reporting has exacerbated the situation. As a result, a badly informed public has no idea what an overrun is, how and why it happens, and what or who is responsible for it. Cost overruns are not new, but they have been greatly aggravated by political considerations and the more sophisticated needs of the government, by its greater dependence on industry, and—most significant—by changes in the government's procurement policies and practices.

Congress, industry, and government acquisition personnel are on a collision course. For competitive procurement valued at $2 million or more, it may take approximately two years from the time a procurement office receives a procurement request until the contract is awarded. Many industrial firms have failed because of inadequate procurement staffs; others have lost procurements for the same reason. But no major private corporation could survive if every procurement worth $2 million or more took the same amount of time it takes the government.

Satisfying the government's high-tech requirements and high-cost systems is a monumental task; the task is compounded by the ever-present need for highly specialized workers. Industry, in addition to having to secure the skilled labor, has to maintain adequate sales to support it. The government, on the other hand, has failed to establish a method for stabilizing sales of major products and has failed to set up a system of rewards when government agencies effect those savings during the procurement process. Changes are essential if we are to secure and maintain superior defense. The government procurement agency proposed in this book is only one method; while such changes take time, it is time to begin.

1.
The Meaning of Cost Overruns and Cost Growth

The government's total procurement budget is approximately $200 billion annually, and the top 200 government contractors receive approximately 90% of that amount. (Small businesses receive approximately 4%, or $8 billion.) In the 1950s, cost overruns accrued at approximately 20% of the total annual procurement dollars per year. Today, that percentage is approximately 65% annually overall. Cost overruns and cost growth (those cost increases due to policy changes) are not new, but their magnitude and percentage in relation to total available procurement dollars have become stifling.

A cost overrun theoretically applies only to cost-reimbursement and fixed-price-incentive and not to firm-fixed price contracts and is the result of an increase in a cost element—material, labor, overhead, general and administrative expense—above that originally quoted without any change in requirements. Typically, an overrun on cost-reimbursement or incentive contracts is the result of an increase in "pooled indirect costs"—fringe benefits, overhead, general and administrative expenses, costs of preparing the bid (B&P), and costs of independent research and development (IR&D)—rather than direct costs such as labor and material.

Outside Washington, a cost overrun is simply—and accurately—referred to as an increase in estimated costs under a cost-reimbursement contract without any change in contract requirements. If actual costs for a cost-reimbursement contract exceed estimated costs without a change in the task to be performed, the contractor is theoretically not entitled to any fee on that portion of the increase approved between estimated and actual costs. Suppose, for example, a contractor bid an estimated cost of $500,000 and a fee of 8% ($40,000) for a cost-reimbursement contract. If actual costs were $1 million when the contract was completed, the contractor's fee would be 4% rather than 8% ($40,000 divided by $1 million), as contractor is not entitled to a fee on the extra $500,000.

In Washington, however, a cost overrun is discussed in terms of "cost," "program cost growth," "program overruns," "increases due to inflation," and "pure program increase"—terms that obfuscate the cause of the program overrun/cost growth and do not address the theoretical definition of "cost overrun." The typical answers outside Washington to "What constitutes an overrun?"—an increase in indirect rates or an increase in direct labor hours and dollars resulting in an increase in the estimated cost of a cost-reimbursement contract—might not be considered overruns in Washington. And neither answer emphasizes the fact that for a fixed-price contract (assuming the requirements do not change), the contractor must deliver the product or service at the agreed-upon price. Nor do they consider constructive changes (those resulting from changes in specifications, for example) or equitable adjustments (those attributable to what a contractor believes he should receive as a result of delays and lost profits, for example). Furthermore, any interpretation of "cost overrun" must emphasize the significance of overall actual program costs in relation to the amount funded.

Overruns by any definition have been a thorn in the nation's economy. They have caused a drastic cutback in the nation's preparedness by forcing a reduction in the number of contracts the government can pursue in any given fiscal year. They have hurt small businesses in particular, because the programs suitable for such businesses are the first to be sacrificed when an overrun occurs on a program for which significant sums have been expended. Greed and selfishness have been rewarded at the expense of efficient, well-managed firms, and competition has been reduced to the point where it is nonexistent. And the Competition in Contracting Act of 1984, implemented April 1, 1985, and intended to increase competition, is not likely to change the situation: Over the years, contracts involving sizable program overruns were awarded for political and economic reasons rather than on the basis of cost or a firm's technical and managerial capabilities and is likely to continue. Thus, the military-industrial complex as "coined" by President Eisenhower is really a "political-military-industrial" complex.

Because major programs are funded through specific appropriation bills, congressional action is required for any additional funding that might be necessary as a result of changes in specifications, deliveries, and quantities. Such congressional actions require separate programming and budgeting by the respective departments, and to consider such cost increases as part of an overrun is grossly misleading.[1] Also misleading is the assumption that inflation is in large measure responsible for increased program costs: Any firm bidding on a multiyear program must take into consideration anticipated increases in costs of labor, material, and other elements, and DCAA is responsible for working with defense contractors to negotiate "advance bidding rates" for multiyear contracts. With few exceptions, inflation has generally been within industry's expectations.

Even if cost overruns per se were not involved the cost

---

1. Using an extended delivery period as the basis for increasing contract costs appears to be another method of covering up a cost overrun, as the original delivery schedule more than likely was unrealistic.

for a radar system, navigation aid or fighter plane would be considerably higher than in 1950.

What, then, accounts for higher costs today than in 1950? Why does a fighter plane, for example, today cost $40 million, whereas a fighter plane in 1950 cost $250,000? Aside from the higher technology involved, *a significant portion of the increase is the result of changes in basic government procurement policy and the treatment of costs.* Price increases that can be attributed solely to a change in procurement policy therefore are hereafter referred to as "cost growth."

In the mid-1950s, for example, the Air Force adopted the concept of weapons systems procurement rather than component procurement. Instead of the government's contracting with various manufacturers of components, who would supply the components to the airframe manufacturer for assembly and installation, the government would award a contract to the prime contractor for the delivery of a fully equipped plane. In the early 1960s, this concept gave way to the concept of total package procurement: The government would award a contract to a prime contractor to supply the airplane and everything needed (ground-handling and checkout equipment) to operate and maintain the aircraft. The prime contractors' tremendous need for engineers to assume the functions formerly performed by Air Force engineers and the numerous tiers of subcontracting and cumulative indirect costs and profits significantly accelerated the price of the aircraft—the cost growth—to the government.

These changes in policy resulted in a greater concentration and more control of government programs and dollars in large corporations. At the same time, they fostered the implementation of two sets of rules, regulations, and procedures—one for small-to-medium firms and another for large corporations. These changes were accompanied by the decentralization of the contract administration and audit functions in the various agencies within the Department of Defense, severely reducing the authority of procurement personnel and fragmenting the procurement process. Contract administration, for example, was transferred to the Defense Contract Administration Services (established in 1965) and made part of the Defense Supply Agency. In December 1964, the Defense Contract Audit Agency was established to assume responsibility for audits, reporting directly to the Secretary of Defense. It began operations July 1, 1965. With its establishment the function of the cost analyst was, for all practical purposes, abolished. In August 1970, the Cost Accounting Standards Board (CASB) was established to eliminate excessively flexible interpretations of ways to measure and record contract costs. Instead of facilitating matters, however, these groups, with the aid of various government boards of contract appeals and the courts, have tended to ignore agreed-upon terms and conditions and generally accepted business and accounting practices—all to the detriment of the nation and its taxpayers.

Exacerbating the situation is the departments' practice of diverting funds not earmarked for a specific program to major programs already approved by Congress so that unused monies do not have to be returned to the Treasury Department. The practice simply leads to abuses, assisting contractors whose program costs have increased to cover the increase without going through normal congressional budgeting channels. If the practice plays havoc with large firms' planning, it is a thousand times more severe for small firms doing business with the government, as they are more vulnerable and more likely to be dropped or postponed indefinitely when a large program experiences overruns or cost growth.

The composition of cost increases has changed significantly since the 1950s. In the 1950s, for example, 60% of increased costs could be attributed to increases in indirect rates and in costs of material and direct labor. Today, however, it is estimated the treatment of costs generally, coupled with cost growth resulting from changes in the government's procurement policy together account for 45% of the increased cost of defense contracts, and they are two areas where the government could save substantial funds. While industry and DCAA might show that indirect rates have decreased since the 1950s, that decrease is more likely to have occurred because of a change in the base and/or the expense pool used in the computation of rates.

TABLE 1
Factors Accounting for Increased Cost of Defense Contracts

	1950s	1980s
Equitable Claims	5%	10%
Tangible Engineering Changes	20%	5%
Fraud	5%	5%
Get Well	10%	20%
Overruns — Increase in Indirect Rates	40% ⎫	⎫
Overruns — Increase in Material and		15% ⎬
Direct Labor other than Get Well	20% ⎭	⎭
Treatment of Costs (Cost Growth)	-0-	20%
Changes in Procurement Policy (Cost Growth)	-0-	25%
	100%	100%

The government has historically refused to take the corrective steps available to it under contract—default, for example—to compel a contractor to mend its ways. Compounding the situation is Congress's approving funds to underwrite government contractors when they run into difficulty on a major project—without a detailed audit of the contractor's financial record to make certain the difficulty was attributable to its government, not its commercial, business.

When such a project runs into difficulties, the government should not be party to withholding those facts about the difficulties from the public but should instead, hold management of those firms accountable. Taxpayers should not be required to pay for the contractors' errors and mismanagement.

The following chapter compares procurement methods and procedures of the 1950s with those of today as a way to explain the increased magnitude of cost overruns and cost growth.

2.
Historical Changes in Major Aspects of Government Procurement

The Magnitude of the Government's Procurement Program

In the fiscal year ending September 30, 1987, the U.S. government initiated approximately 22.3 million procurement actions, whose total value was $197.3 billion. The approximate breakdown for the Department of Defense (DOD) and other agencies is shown in table 2 which follows.

TABLE 2
Number of Procurement Actions and Dollars*

	Total Actions	Total Dollars (billions)
Department of Defense		
$25,000 and over	253,749	$141.4
Under $25,000	15,047,108	14.0
All Other Agencies		
$25,000 and over	161,983	37.2
Under $25,000	6,836,766	4.7

*Source: Federal Procurement Data System, Standard Report, Fiscal Year 1987 (October 1, 1986, through September 30, 1987).

NOTES:
(1) Any procurement action with a value of $25,000 or more requires a formal contract.
(2) Current legislation authorizes procurement actions of under $10,000 to be handled expeditiously. While anything under $25,000 is considered a "small" purchase, purchases between $10,000 and $25,000 must follow a more time-consuming route than those below $10,000.

The number of actions and their value are staggering. They are even more impressive when one considers that in fiscal year 1987 small purchases (those under $25,000) accounted for as much as the government's entire procurement budget in 1951 ($18.3 billion).[2]

In 1951, the gross national product (GNP) was $324.4 billion, the federal government expended $57.8 billion, and federal procurement purchases accounted for $18.5 billion, or 5.7% of the GNP. In 1984 with a significant increase in GNP ($3.6 trillion) and federal government expenditures ($852 billion), federal procurement purchases still accounted for approximately 5% ($183 billion) of GNP.

More important, however, is the fact that procurement practices in 1951 were completely different from those of the 1980s. Most changes since 1951 have dissipated the authority of the government's contract specialists—the government's buyers—by assigning their responsibilities to others and by diluting their control of costs and performance—which in turn, directly or indirectly resulted in an increased overrun or cost growth for almost every item acquired by the government.

Procurement Policy

Early 1950s. In the early 1950s, many large corporations, still recovering from the effects of World War II, were attempting to reestablish themselves in commercial markets. The government's procurement budget was very small, and

2. The numerous changes in small purchases since 1951 affect the price the government pays for its goods and services. The floor, for example, has been raised from $10,000 to $25,000, and all purchases of $10,000 or less are reserved for small businesses, which generally means going to a distributor or wholesaler rather than a manufacturer, although the government could secure a better price by going to the manufacturer. For architectural/engineering requirements, quotations up to $2,000 can be verbal. For other requirements, anything up to $1,000 can be verbal, and only one supplier need bid. While the greatest number of transactions is probably $1,000 and under, the federal procurement data system, which accumulates data on procurement actions, breaks out information only in the categories of "under $25,000" and "over $25,000." It would be more meaningful to break down procurement actions according to the processing required by the applicable procurement regulations, so that the dollar categories of the small purchases with the greatest number of actions would be readily apparent. Changes in procedures could result in further savings in the area of small purchases.

the electronics and aerospace industries were insignificant. Government engineers prepared detailed specifications or performance specifications for the various components of an aircraft or a weapons sysem, and the government procured each component directly from the manufacturer. When it received the components, the government then assembled the system in-house or had a private firm integrate the system. Aircraft companies, under the component procurement system, were essentially airframe developers and fabricators and aircraft assemblers, and they were responsible for approximately 70% of the total cost of an airplane.

The system was not without its faults—delays in delivery of components by suppliers, scheduling problems, overly cumbersome government procurement regulations.

Late 1950s. The concept of weapons system procurement was introduced in the late 1950s for the purpose of shifting the responsibility for the operational success of a complex system from the government to a prime contractor, simplifying negotiations, and saving the government time and money. The prime contractor now became responsible for delivering a "radar system" or an "airplane," for example, and the government's need for engineers, maintenance personnel, and repair facilities diminished. The prime contractor now assumed responsibility for engineering, manufacturing, assembling, and delivering a fully equipped airplane. In the process, it was decided, government agencies no longer needed the specialized in-depth engineering expertise associated with the numerous ancillary items, and this capability was dispersed.

Award of the first contracts for weapons systems proved the government could not overcome problems of interface and scheduling simply by awarding of a contract, however. Aircraft manufacturers now had to acquire all the technical expertise formerly contained within the Air Force and its suppliers, and early contracts for weapons systems contained significantly higher costs. More important, the government's switch stifled competition and caused havoc in the industry. Many suppliers that had dealt directly with the government found themselves in an entirely new game. For many of the smaller firms, the government had been their only customer, but now they had to deal with system contractors that were horizontally integrated, accustomed to manufacturing only the airframe and overall assembly, and unable to write and monitor complex procurement specifications for components and subsystems without qualified technical personnel. Thus, the component, subassembly, and subsystem suppliers were confronted with two choices: play ball and supply all the information the prime contractor wanted—in essence giving away trade secrets—or sell out. Many elected to sell out.

Pressure on the subcontractors from the prime system contractors was not restricted to the technical area; it was equally, if not more, harsh in audits and price negotiations. Terms and conditions in the prime contract—progress payments made to the prime contractor, for example—were not always passed on to subcontractors. And because systems were becoming more sophisticated, subcontracting now amounted to approximately 50% of the selling price to the government, up from 30%.

The system procurement concept ushered in the era of the program manager/project manager and project office. It served as a transition time for the transfer of the government's expertise and the writing of its system specifications to industry and nonprofit think tanks. And it permitted weapons systems contractors to enter technical areas formerly dominated by other firms.

1960s to Today. As systems became more complex and larger, the need for ground-handling and check-out equipment became more acute. The result was the concept of total package procurement, in which the systems contractor was also responsible for check-out equipment and for maintenance and repair. Thus, between 1951 and 1984, the government permitted its in-house technical capability to be depleted, and subcontracting on major systems rose from approximately 30% of the selling price in the early 1950s to 50% in the late 1950s to 70% in the 1960s. Recognizing the total package procurement concept was too expensive, the government cut back on the use of that concept, but subcontracting remains in the 50%-70% range.

In fiscal year 1987, as a result, the top 200 government contractors accounted for approximately 90%—$177 billion —of the government's total procurement budget of $197 billion. Because approximately 50%, on average, of the government's total procurement budget is subcontracted by these prime contractors, the cost growth resulting from the multiple layers of contractors' costs for overhead, materials handling, and general and administrative expense and for profit is significant. And the situation is even unhealthier from the standpoint of national security in that the industrial base has shrunk considerably in the past 10 years —a period during which procurement expenditures increased significantly.

Changes in Procurement Policy and Their Effect on Process and Price

The increase in subcontracting is not solely at fault, however. Numerous other changes, when combined with this degree of subcontracting, have been devastating: inadequate procurement specifications, contractual terms and conditions that ensure a contractor's reimbursement for its costs, whatever they are, or political pressure to settle a claim without adequate supporting cost data. Such practices have made firms in the government marketplace so lax that they have forgotten how to be competitive. The facts speak for themselves. The shipbuilding, steel, electronics, and aerospace industries—key industries for the defense of this nation—are all hurting.

Table 3 shows the cumulative costs for all goods and services purchased in 1987 under contracts (i.e., those over $25,000) and compares them to what the same goods and services would have cost if they had been purchased in 1951. Why the disparity in selling price between 1951 and 1987? The difference lies in subcontracting, fringe benefits, and the treatment of materials handling and general and administrative expense.

TABLE 3
Consolidated Cost Breakdown—All Goods and Services
1987 versus 1951
(billions of dollars)

	1987	1951		
		Subcontracted Parts	In-house Effort	Total
	(1)	(2)	(3)	(4)
1. MATERIALS				
a. Subcontracting	$ 70.0	$70.0		$ 70.0
b. Parts	20.0	20.0		20.0
c. Raw Material	10.0		10.0	10.0
d. TOTAL MATERIALS	$100.0	$90.0	$10.0	$100.0
2. MATERIALS HANDLING	2.0	.9		.9
	(2% of Line 1d)	(1% of Line 1d)		
3. DIRECT LABOR (D/L)	6.5		6.5	6.5
4. FRINGE BENEFITS	2.6		.3	.3
	(40% of D/L)		(5% of D/L)	
5. TOTAL DIRECT LABOR	9.1		6.8	6.8
(Line 3 + 4)				
6. OVERHEAD	25.0		18.7	18.7
(275% of Line 5)				
7. COST OF GOODS SOLD	136.1	90.9	35.5	126.4
(Lines 1 through 4 + 6)				
8. OTHER DIRECT COSTS	5.0	N/A		N/A
9. TOTAL COST INPUT	141.1			126.4
(Line 7 + 8)				
10. GENERAL & ADMINISTRATIVE EXPENSE				
a. G&A (20%)				
b. IR&D (4%)		included in overhead and/or G&A		
c. B&P (6%)		included in overhead and/or G&A		
TOTAL G&A	42.3		3.6	3.6
	(30% of Line 9)		(10% of Line 7)	
11. SUBTOTAL	183.4	90.9	39.1	130.0
12. PROFIT	22.0	.5	3.9	4.4
	(12% of Line 11)	(0.5% of Line 11)	(10% of Line 11)	
13. SELLING PRICE	$205.4	$91.4	$43.0	$134.4
(Line 11 + 12)				

The irony of procurement today is that, with a considerably higher procurement expenditure, the government buyer is for the most part kept out of the picture until a procurement request—the document authorizing a procurement—is received in the procurement office, even though the Federal Acquisition Regulation requires advance procurement planning—a complete reversal of past practices; and, for major programs, members of Congress, the administration, secretaries of departments, project office personnel, industry representatives, and procurement office personnel are supposed to cooperate. The question is, do they communicate with the buyer as the requirement progresses through the system?

The technology involved and the scope and dollar value of projects today are magnitudes greater than they were in the 1950s. Many more firms than were available in the 1950s are capable of satisfying the government's needs in most technical areas. Thus it is even more imperative that sound procurement practices be reintroduced and implemented. A good place to start would be to reverse the government's practice of subordinating procurement personnel to personnel in the project or program office.

Government Personnel and Their Responsibilities

The most far-reaching changes in the procurement field since 1951 have been in the area of government personnel and their responsibilities. At one time, the government had not only the engineering talent and expertise to prepare procurement specifications and work statements but also the necessary facilities to test finished products; but today the government must rely heavily on industry and nonprofit organizations for the preparation of specifications and for the testing and evaluation of various systems. Furthermore, in the early 1950s, the government could require that applicants for a

procurement position have a college degree. Sin‹
ever, the Office of Personnel Management has c
curement personnel as "administrative" rather t‹
sional." Accordingly, a college degree is no lon₋₋₋ required
for the government's buyers—who must nonetheless be
knowledgeable about a multitude of areas (statutes, regulations, practices and procedure, and legal, technical, business, and accounting issues). This requirement for "professional" knowledge in an "administrative" position is a major
barrier to the government's securing an adequate purchasing
staff. And it reflects the government's position that procurement is a "service" function, subservient to other functions.
When tens of billions of dollars are involved, it would appear
that procurement personnel should be regarded more highly.

Several key government personnel are likely to be
involved in procurement.

Director, Office of Contracts. The person responsible
for managing and supervising all activities in a procurement
office; has a contracting officer's warrant.

Contracting Officer (CO). A person having authority to
obligate the government contractually. This authority is
usually vested in the head of an agency and is delegated to
others in the organization. A procurement office may contain
numerous contracting officers, for example, the director of
procurement and supervisory contract specialists. In some
offices, the delegation of the contracting officer's authority
extends further down the organization. The warrants issued
to the various contracting officers cite specific limitations—
for example, the type of contract, product(s), or services, and
limits on the amount of funding. The CO has the final say in
the matter and, by signing a contract, states that the price
offered is fair and reasonable.

Contracting officers are further classified as *procurement contracting officers* (PCOs, or simply COs in civil agencies) (those at a headquarters or prime commodity purchasing office), *administrative contracting officers* (ACOs) (those performing administrative functions at procurement offices or contract administration offices like the Defense Logistics Agency's Defense Contract Administration Services Management Area [DCASMA] offices), or *termination contracting officers* (TCOs) (those who settle terminated contracts).

PCOs have specific authority to sign off on contracts, to negotiate and make new contract awards, and in many instances to administer the contract as well. Depending on the agency; the PCO might also negotiate and award all modifications to the basic contract (usually the case for civil agencies).

ACOs are located in those prime commodity or headquarters procurement offices where procurement is divided into two responsibilities—those who negotiate and award contracts and those who administer contracts. For DOD, the ACO in a DCASMA office, after securing the DCAA auditor's report for the contractor's indirect cost proposal, negotiates indirect rates with the contractor. (In civil agencies, these rates are advisory.) Some departments in DOD might permit the ACO in DCASMA to negotiate contract modifications up to a certain value.

Today, a serious question is raised as to who is responsible for negotiating the price and terms of a contract—the buyer (PCO), the auditor (from DCAA), the ACO, the project manager, or the Inspector General (IG).

TCOs are generally located at a prime commodity or headquarters procurement office.

Supervisory Contract Specialist. Generally, a contracting officer assigned to supervise the work of one or more contract specialists.

Contract Specialist. A government buyer engaged in awarding formal contracts—those valued at $25,000 or more. This individual may or may not have a contracting officer's warrant.

Contract Negotiator. A title (rather than contract specialist) assigned to an individual who negotiates a contract and then turns it over to an administrative contracting officer.

Contract Administrator. An individual who performs contract administration; may or may not have a contracting officer's warrant.

Purchasing Agent. A person who handles small purchases—those for which the aggregate amount does not exceed $25,000. These purchases result in the award of a purchase order rather than a formal contract, and the purchasing agent may or may not have a contracting officer's warrant.

Program Manager, Project Manager, Contracting Officer's Technical Representative, Contract Technical Manager. The personnel responsible for researching and defining the technical requirements to satisfy an agency's need, developing a cost estimate for budgetary and procurement purposes, preparing the statement of work and/or the procurement specification, writing the procurement request (the procurement authorization document), evaluating technical proposals, assisting the contract specialist in determining the reasonableness of prices, and monitoring the contractor's performance. These personnel do not have the authority to obligate the government.

Auditor. The auditor's functions are varied and extensive, including verifying how the contractor quotes, records, and bills costs and whether internal procedures are in fact complied with. What the auditor looks for depends upon the type of audit requested. For example, if a preaward assist audit has been requested, the auditor might want to review the contractor's accounting system (if the accounting system has never been audited) to determine its adequacy for the segregation, accumulation, and recording of costs under the contemplated contract. The auditor might want to verify quoted hourly labor rates as current and applicable, in which case the government might bring in a quality assurance or production specialist.

The predominant audit group in the government is the Defense Contract Audit Agency. Although it is part of the Department of Defense, it is also responsible for most of the audits for civil agencies.

Today, auditors are more often being asked to analyze costs, despite the fact that most do not have the required background to perform a cost analysis. An auditor's function is to verify that costs are treated in accordance with established procedures, regulations, guidelines, and/or generally accepted accounting practices. The function of a cost analyst, however, is to look at reported costs to determine their fairness and reasonableness, and this function is completely different from that of an auditor.

Contract Cost Analyst. The person in a major procurement office who assists the contract specialist to evaluate a contractor's cost proposal and determine whether the price quoted is fair and reasonable. In the process, the cost analyst contacts the cognizant audit group to confirm the contractor's indirect cost rates. (Indirect costs account for approximately 35-65% of the selling price of a procurement; they include fringe benefits, overhead, general and administrative expense, expense of preparing the bid and proposal, independent research and development, and cost of money—all of which DCAA auditors monitor and negotiate.) For large defense contracts, the rates recommended and negotiated by DCAA are firm—a fairly recent development, as the rates were formerly negotiated by the DCASMARO, ACO, and, before that, by the various government buyers.

Quality Assurance/Production Specialist. The person who reviews a firm's facilities and capabilities; may be part of the agency involved or part of a DCASMA office.

Industrial Property Officer. The government personnel assigned to monitor the issuance and delivery of government-furnished property or contractor-acquired property.

Organization for Procurement

Over the years, the titles of government procurement personnel have not changes. What has changed are the roles and places of authority in the organizations they work for. The result has been a distrust for personnel in one group as to what "the other government group" is doing. In many instances, this distrust is justified, as some government groups are extremely lax and simply do not comply with applicable statutes, regulations, procedures, and practices. Even though one government department or agency may have a major investment in a program procured by another government agency, the first group might be precluded from observing first-hand what is happening on the project. And most of these internal government conflicts tend to benefit industry. Is this second look a duplication of effort? Yes. Is it desirable? Absolutely.

In its final report, the President's Blue Ribbon Commission on Defense Management, chaired by David Packard, recommended the establishment of an under secretary of defense for acquisition to work full time on acquisition matters. But, because the new position covers all aspects of acquisition—including research, development, advanced technology, test and evaluation, and cost assessment as well as acquisition policy and procurement—procurement personnel remain subservient to program or project office personnel. And the major deficiency in the government's present procurement arrangement would remain.

Rather than be subservient to program, project, or administrative personnel, the procurement office should have a direct line to the relevant secretary's office. If project personnel are not doing their job, they should be held accountable. Rather than proceed with a procurement with inadequate specifications, for example, personnel should be compelled to correct the deficiencies—a situation that is almost impossible at the present time.

In the 1950s, procurement personnel had greater independence in the procurement process. Each department in DOD, for example, had its own buyers, auditors, production specialists, contract administration support staff, and so on, and each department's procurement function was controlled by the department itself. The many organizational changes since the 1950s—establishment of the Defense Contract Audit Agency, the Defense Supply Agency later superseded by the Defense Logistics Agency [DLA] and, under it, the Defense Contract Administration Services Agency, and the Cost Accounting Standards Board—created a situation comparable to that of a surgeon's bringing in a substitute during a critical operation.

The movement has not been confined to government. Since the 1950s, many contractors have established specialized groups to respond to government solicitations, especially for R&D projects, and upon award of a contract would hand the job to other groups. Invariably the group assigned the project after award of the contract would disagree with the approach taken. Today this is a major problem area, as the major programs entail diverse technical disciplines.

Thus, the negotiation and administration of contracts between industry and the government are in no way standardized: Some contracts remain the responsibility of the PCO from beginning to end, whereas others are turned over to an ACO sometime after award. This split in responsibilities has resulted in a duplication of effort. From a legal standpoint, it raises the question of who is responsible for what. According to government regulations, for example, the government buyer (contract specialist) is solely responsible for determining the reasonableness of the quoted price. An entirely different impression, however, is created by the language of contract clauses, Cost Accounting Standards, disclosure statements, DCAA's audit reports, and statutes and regulations concerning the resolution of audit findings. To compound an already bad situation, more and more congressmen and other government personnel now want personnel in DCAA and the Office of the Inspector General—the same personnel responsible for the present failed state of the procurement process—to take an even more active role in procurement, further diluting the buyer's position. This situation can lead to even further erosion, since DCAA's present staff is incapable of performing timely and meaningful audits.

The standards promulgated by the CASB permit a company to set up an unrealistic number of cost centers for the accumulation and establishment of indirect rates, without any regard to generally accepted accounting practices and without considering whether or not the cost center should be authorized if the costs contribute to and benefit the entire company, not just a single contract. The result is that engineering, testing, technical publications, machining, quality control, research and development, and many more areas could be treated as subcontractors in a corporation, each with its own indirect rate structure and applicable profit.

Procurement Requests and Specifications
The preparation of the procurement requests and specif-

cations is the most critical area of the acquisition process, and the government has elected to rely on industry for this function having dispersed its in-house technical capability.

In the 1950s when a procurement request was submitted to the procurement office for action, it was logged in and then assigned to a buyer. If the request was incomplete or the specifications considered inadequate, it was likely to be returned for revision. With today's number and size of jobs, the need is even greater that specifications be complete and written for the method of procurement (formal advertisement, contract awarded to low bidder, or negotiated contract) and type of contract (fixed price or cost reimbursement). The possibility of a procurement requests being returned for rework if it is deficient is virtually nonexistent, however, for several reasons: Buyers have been instructed to assume the responsiblility for filling in the gaps and are discouraged from returning the request to the originator because of time constraints imposed by statutes and regulations. The foregoing ignores the fact that most buyers do not have the training or knowledge to recognize deficiencies in the procurement requests and specifications.

A related problem concerns the use of commercial products to satisfy the government's needs. Before specifying a commercial product, the project engineer must cite the minimum technical requirements to satisfy the government's solicitation, a task considerably more difficult today than it was in the 1950s. The reason? The government relies more on industry and has depleted its technical expertise. And because specifications are inadequate, industry essentially has a blank check to produce its product. Furthermore, government's philosophy appears to be that it wants a product—at whatever cost.

Project personnel are lax in specifying contractual requirements: items to be delivered, delivery schedule, shipping instructions, terms for inspection and acceptance, FOB point, option to extend period of performance, government-furnished equipment or government-furnished property, and warranties. The result is that approximately half of all requests are submitted prematurely, and the outcome is inefficiency, decreased production, and bad contracts. And the price is steep. An inadequate procurement package submitted to industry for a quotation could result in 20 or more amendments to the solicitation and could mean two or three years before a contract is awarded.

To alleviate that situation, a new job classification for senior procurement personnel—Procurement Planning/Coordination Specialist—should be established. That person should have the proper education, training, and experience to work with key agency personnel, to develop the method of procurement, contract type, and sources, and to oversee the writing of the specifications and procurement request—all to ensure that the package is adequate before it is even submitted to procurement. Further, the Procurement Planning/Coordination Specialist should be able to approve procurements over $2 million—the function currently performed by a source evaluation board that adds six months to two years to the process.

Today, as in the 1950s, government acquisition personnel have to contend with industry salesmanship, but they are less equipped to handle it.

Competition

Approximately 85% of the government's total procurement budget is awarded as a result of negotiated procurements; probably about 90% of those dollars are the result of sole-source negotiated procurements (where only one source is invited to bid). Since 1951, those figures have remained virtually constant. On April 1, 1985, however, the implementation of the Competition in Contracting Act (CICA) significantly changed procurement regulations by reducing the number of exemptions from a competitive award to 7 rather than 17 for DOD and 15 for civil agencies. At the same time, the government made it easier for firms to compete. Accordingly, the number of competitive negotiated procurements will increase significantly. But how meaningful are these numbers? At best, they serve as window dressing.

In the past, even though the time and effort expended to evaluate small-value R&D proposals was often more than the amount of the contract, small businesses were still able to participate. Since the implementation of CICA, however, government agencies have established a trend of consolidating several requirements, including R&D, that will prevent small businesses from competing because they do not have the resources to perform the expanded tasks. The result of the consolidation is a decrease in the number of procurement actions and less competition. Another practice that will manifest itself is the use of bidders lists comprising other than true competitors, resulting in an increase in the number of "complementary" bids submitted at the request of the procurement office for the sole purpose of feigning competition. And with the feigned competition, more reliance will be placed on price analysis rather than cost analysis. Price analysis does not require a detailed cost breakdown and analysis and opens the door to "buy-ins" (contractors that intentionally understate costs to gain an undue price advantage) and other abuses. These practices can only increase the cost of the resultant contracts. (Cost versue price analysis is discussed in more detail in the next section.)

Although it may appear that many firms can satisfy the government's requirements, that appearance is illusory. A multitude of firms in the micorcomputer field, for example, could supply the basic requirements, but the number with the networking, interface, and interchange capability is limited.

Negotiations

Another significant change in procurement since the 1950s has been in the area of negotiations—particularly with respect to the information available to buyers, the treatment of costs, and the role of auditors.

In the 1950s, each major department within DOD had its own supporting field staff, which included auditors. Audits today are performed by the Defense Contract Audit Agency, a separate agency within DOD, and individual departments have lost control of this important aspect of the procurement process.

In the 1950s, almost all negotiated procurements were subject to cost analysis. Often, two or more proposals for a single requirement were analyzed to determine which was the most realistic and best offer for the government. If the criteria used in the 1950s were still in use in the 1980s, a minimum of approximately 4% (16,600 actions over $100,000 in value) of the 415,732 contract actions awarded in 1987 would be subject to cost analysis. Only about 2,500 actions were in fact subjected to a detailed cost analysis, however. Further, if Congress passes a bill that the Senate approved in mid-1986, S. 2433, authorizing the simplified competitive acquisition technique (SCAT), the number of procurement actions subjected to cost analysis will drop to fewer than 2,500 governmentwide. SCAT would eliminate the need for a cost analysis and preaward assist audit on all competitively negotiated contracts valued at under $1 million, rather than under the $5 million floor recommended by the administration.

To secure adequate cost data and to negotiate the terms of a contract take time, but government buyers in the 1950s generally had the support of their superiors in obtaining the necessary data. Since then, government buyers have lost that support for lengthy negotiations. Accordingly, more and more agencies have turned to price analysis rather than cost analysis. (Cost analysis requires a detailed cost breakdown from the offeror—the contractor—which is reviewed by a cost analyst, who evaluates the quoted cost element to determine if, for example, the types of personnel, hourly rates, material etc. are reasonable for the products or services being purchased. The cost analyst then makes the necessary cost adjustments and recommends a price to the buyer.) But regardless of the dollars involved, government procurement regulations do not require a cost breakdown if the contract is expected to be based on price analysis, which assumes "adequate competition"; that is, it assumes that two or more contractors who are determined to meet the requirements, will submit independent proposals. Price analysis involves evaluating the offerors' technical compliance, performance, delivery, and other factors and then looking at the price to determine the successful bidder. This approach increases the cost of a program by approximately 20%. No substitute exists for negotiations based on detailed financial statements and cost breakdowns.

Government policy downplaying the importance of cost analysis commenced with the establishment of DCAA at which time cost analysts were absorbed into the organization as price analysts and the function of the cost analyst evaporated. It is a carryover from the Defense Acquisition Regulation (DAR) and the Armed Services Procurement Regulation (ASPR), predecessors to the FAR. FAR Part 15.803 (d) states, "The contracting officer's primary concern is the price the government actually pays; the contractor's eventual cost and profit or fee should be a secondary concern." This policy is restated in the Armed Services Pricing Manual (ASPM), DOD 1986, page 2-8, which reads,

"Government procurement is concerned primarily with the reasonableness of the price which the Government ultimately pays, and only secondarily with the eventual cost and profit to the contractor."

In the 1950s, on negotiated procurements over $100,000, a supplier had to submit its latest financial statements (profit and loss statement and balance sheet) with its proposal. Today, major contractors often are not requested to submit such financial statements to the buyer or to DCAA auditors (although small suppliers generally are).

In the 1950s, government cost analysts would use those financial statements to compute the indirect rates applicable to the pending procurement so that the government's buyer would have detailed cost data for negotiations. Today, the DCAA audit report often includes no back-up data about how the rates were determined and no comments about the contractor—its normal business, the dollar value of its sales, whether additional personnel will be necessary, whether its accounting system is adequate to accumulate, segregate, and record costs, or the possible effect of the pending procurement on the contractor's indirect cost rates. Sales volume, a key factor in determining indirect costs for commercial business activity, has been determined to be irrelevant for the government's costing purposes. The importance of this information cannot be overstated, however, when one considers that government requirements generally fall into one of four broad categories, all of which entail different cost structures: research and development, manufacturing, services (repair and maintenance of equipment and buildings and preparation of technical publications), and construction. In the 1950s, when detailed information on indirect costs was available, a government buyer could negotiate with a supplier of radar, for example, a different rate structure for the indirect costs for each task.

Industry did not like that situation, arguing that confidential financial statements could fall into the wrong hands. Further, it argued, using different indirect rates for different types of requirements and for different agencies was unfair. As a result, when DCAA was established, major government contractors were successful in limiting government buyers' access to their financial records and cost data. Today, the government is at the mercy of its major contractors regarding their financial condition and the establishment of cost centers. A buyer cannot determine whether a cost center is logical and proper: that information is controlled by the auditor, not by the buyer.

Even though a firm's sales play a significant role when one is estimating the firm's direct and indirect costs and the resultant anticipated profits, government auditors today are not concerned with major suppliers' dollar volumes of sales. Government regulations—Cost Accounting Standards, Contract Cost Principles, DCAA's practices—focus on expense pools and on the bases that form the different indirect cost rates for the cost centers of contractors performing government business. Without knowledge of sales, however, buyers work in a vacuum. Further, they do not have to consider a contractor's commercial business, costing for which is significantly different from costing for its government business or company-sponsored research. Compounding this situation is the fact that nothing in the government regulations or practices states that the costs of any commercial business housed within the same facility as government business must be treated the same way as the costs of government business or that government auditors have access to these data.

This situation is startling: The dollar volume of business within a facility directly affects indirect costs, which account for 35-65% of the selling price to the government. Further, sales volume also bears on direct costs, which affect the indirect cost rate structure. How can an auditor then ignore a firm's sales?

Audit reports seldom cover the use of government-furnished equipment or government-furnished property or a contractor's need for additional facilities to perform the work. Exclusion of this information means that the exercise in costing is meaningless. The government limits the financial and cost reviews of its major suppliers, and covers costs for other than government projects over the annual multibillion-dollar subsidy to its giant contractors through IR&D, B&P and treatment of costs in general (discussed in Chapters 3 and 4).

To control and dominate costs, DCAA has always retained within itself most information concerning the shortcomings and problems with government contractors' accounting systems rather than pass the information onto government buyers, who would be able to use it in negotiations. In so doing, DCAA has infringed on many areas where the buyer should have sole authority and responsibility—the reasonableness of price, for example.

DCAA audit reports have become meaningless, containing little useful information for negotiations. They stress nonallowable, unsupported, and questioned costs without adequately explaining them or indicating that the contractor's accounting system is inadequate for segregating, accumulating, and reporting costs as required by the government. In many instances, procurement personnel are placed in the untenable position of having to ignore the auditor's findings to award the contract and get the job done.

The presence of 6,200 auditors in DCAA does not mean that the government is ensured a reasonable price for its goods and services.

Legal/Cost Problems

Even when a buyer has taken the proper steps to ensure the government's receiving a reasonable price in its purchase of goods and services and has incorporated into the contract specific terms and conditions agreed to during negotiations, contractors have disregarded or contested those terms and conditions. And in all too many instances, the government's Board of Contract Appeals or government officials have supported the contractor. Contributing to this situation since the 1950s has been the government's unwritten self-governance policy which was made "official" subsequent to being recommended in the June 1986 report of the Packard Commission.

The rest of this section lists areas in which deviations from contractually agreed-upon terms and conditions have taken place, at a cost to the government of billions of dollars.

• *Indirect rate schedules and profits for all inter-and intracorporate transactions under a contract.* The more a prime contractor can do within its own corporate structure, the more competitive it should be, simply by virtue of eliminating subcontracts and their attendant indirect costs and profits. Nevertheless, many system contractors have treated inter- and intracompany efforts as subcontracts with all their attendant additional costs, despite having specified in their bids that such efforts would bear one set of indirect rates and a single profit. And when the practice is challenged, the contractor's position is upheld.

Permitting multiple layers of indirect costs and profits adds considerably to the government's costs, given the growth in size of most large government contractors, since the 1950s. Through acquisitions, mergers, and expansions, most large government contractors have become considerably larger. The scope of their capabilities, the number of their plants, and the number of their personnel have grown accordingly.

• **A contractor's ability to change the location where work is performed.** In numerous instances, a contractor has stated in its bid (and the resulting contract repeated) that work would be performed at one plant, and the contractor based its quotation on that location as the FOB point. Subsequently, however, the contractor might have moved the government project to a more costly facility or relocated an unprofitable commercial project or a company-sponsored R&D project to the plant where the government's project was being performed. In all such instances, the contractor's actions increase the cost to the government, but the Board of Contract Appeals has ruled that the government cannot dictate to a company how it will handle its business.

• **Decisions to make or buy under system contracts.** Often a contractor decides to produce an item itself, despite having specified in its bid that that item would be subcontracted. The result is that the government ends up sponsoring the contractor to produce an item that is already developed and/or manufactured by another company—and the cost to the government is exorbitant.

• **Use of the "most-favored customer" clause.** This contract provision asserts that the contractor agrees to grant the government most-favored customer status; that is, the price quoted the government is the same as or lower than that offered to any other customer. Although this clause appears to give the government the protection it needs to ensure a favorable price, that has not in fact happened: Neither the Board of Contract Appeals nor the courts have supported the clause.

• **Government's right to technical data.** Often, when the government sponsors the development of a new product, agency personnel do not enforce contractual requirements that the contractor supply detailed remanufacturing drawings and data. The result is that when the item must be procured again, either a new contractor must reinvent the wheel or the government must rehire the original contractor.

• **Requirements for bills of material for common commercial parts and for specially designed, manufactured parts.** Often contractors refuse to supply detailed information for common, off-the-shelf items—part numbers, government stock numbers, suppliers' names and addresses—and refuse also to supply a separate list with the same data on specially designed and manufactured parts that would enable the government to procure such items directly from the manufacturer and save huge sums of money. For the most part, agency personnel have done nothing to enforce the contractual requirements that such information be supplied.

• **Patent rights.** Even though the government pays for the development of a product, it often does not secure unlimited rights to that product.

• **Submission of requested cost data in time for negotiations.** The greater the costs incurred before a price is agreed upon, the smaller the contractor's risk and accordingly the smaller the profit margin. The practice of not agreeing to price until most work is done is cost-plus-percentage-of-cost contracting and is outlawed; yet the practice is generally followed for most major government programs.

• **Major contractual concessions to contractors.** Government employees have furnished property and equipment to contractors and have converted contract type, terms, and conditions—without adequate consideration. Contractors have thus been able to recover additional monies.

• **The use of socioeconomic programs for small businesses.** With the exception of firms contracted with under the "8a program" for minority and disadvantaged businesses, small businesses do not generally operate in a sole-source environment. They compete with other small businesses if a requirement is set aside for small businesses or with large businesses, which, because of current government costing practices, have an undue advantage. As a result, small businesses often push other small businesses into bankruptcy by underbidding costs.

• **Costing.** present statutes and regulations make auditing almost impossible and ignore practical business considerations, generally accepted accounting practices, and agreements reached during negotiations.

• **Fraud.** The concept of systems procurement opened up a potentially very costly (to the government) area of fraud—instances in which a prime contractor awards subcontracts to firms owned and operated by friends, relatives, or family members, some under assumed or fictitious names. In some cases, payment is made for doing nothing; in others, charges are excessive for the work performed. In too many cases, the government neither audits the prime contractor's subcontracting procedures nor verifies compliance in the work place.

Disregard of Procurement Regulations

The practices cited in the previous section have resulted in the violation or circumvention of procurement statutes and regulations. And government employees' practice of acceding to contractors' wishes during negotiations rather than adhering to sound principles of costing and business practices only exacerbates the matter. Even worse, once the practices get out of hand, a law is passed to make the improper practices legal.

For example:

• The practice of meeting the need for competition by filling lists of bidders with other than true competitors and by preparing inadequate specifications or work statements so that only a bidder working with project personnel can understand what is required can only be expected to become more frequent with passage of the Competition in Contracting Act, which makes it easier for government buyers to use competitive negotiated procurements.

• The need for detailed cost breakdowns on certain procurements is compromised by provisions in the regulations stating that if adequate price competition exists, a detailed cost breakdown is not required. But what constitutes "adequate" price competition? The regulations state only that competition exists if two or more firms bid independently and each shows that it can satisfy the requirements.

Even when detailed cost breakdowns are required, however, a meaningful cost analysis is unlikely. In FY 1987, for example, out of approximately 415,700 formal contract actions, approximately 4% (16,600) were over $100,000 and may have required a detailed cost proposal. Of those 16,600 awards, it is questionable whether even 2,500 were subjected to meaningful cost analysis. Accordingly, the administration, through the Office of Federal Procurement Policy of the Office of Management and Budget, proposed the simplified competitive acquisition technique. Under the administration's proposal, procurements under $5 million for which price competition was adequate would not be subject to a cost breakdown, a cost analysis, or a preaward audit. If that proposal were to become law, fewer than 1,000 quotations would be subject to detailed cost analysis. On June 25, 1986, the Senate approved a modified version of the administration's proposal, S. 2433. Currently, both bills are in consideration. Under the Senate's version of the bill, procurements under $1 million with adequate price competition would not be subject to a cost breakdown, a cost analysis, or a preaward audit. If the House also approves that bill, it will legalize what has been happening throughout the government for years: Approximately 2,500 cost proposals, and no more, will be subject to cost analysis. Without cost analysis, however, no basis exists for negotiations. And even when a cost analysis is performed, it is usually meaningless or terms are not negotiated. With few exceptions, the lack of cost data applies to small purchases as well as to awards over $25,000 (formal contracts).

• The regulations promulgated by the CASB, DCAA, and DLA have infringed on areas formerly the domain of the contracting officer. Through the years, those agencies have assumed roles restricting and conflicting with those of the buyer, greatly undermining the government buyer's position in negotiations. In the past three years, Congress has passed numerous statutes in the procurement area. The fact is that proper, logical action could have been taken by the agencies to correct many of the areas addressed, but was not.

• In 1987, DOD implemented a revised "weighted guidelines method" of determining profits. The regulation curtails the inclusion of general and administrative expense in the calculation of profits, reduces the weighting factor for labor and puts engineering talent on the same level with menial productive labor, and places more emphasis on capital investment, thereby drastically reducing the profit rate by approximately 40% (lowering it from 8% to 5%) for most innovative small R&D firms while reducing profit for major government contractors approximately 9% lowering it from 14% to 13%.

• The Truth in Negotiation Act, P.L. 87-653, has been compromised by both government and industry. The Board of Contract Appeals has generally ruled that if a contracting officer requests specific cost information from a supplier or potential supplier and the information is incorrect, the contractor is liable. All too often, however, the contracting officer does not require a detailed cost breakdown for material, labor, and/or subcontracts, or the contractor has failed to supply detailed data. In that case the contracting officer may rely on information secured by DCAA. But, the Board of Contract Appeals has ruled that information secured by a third party is not data known to the contracting officer and therefore cannot be used against the contractor. Recent legislation may strengthen P.L. 87-653. Today, price analysis offers government buyers a means of circumventing the Truth in Negotiation Act.

• Self-governance on the part of contractors applies to all aspects of the acquisition process, including engineering, billing, costing, testing, quality control, etc., and the result has been an overall watering down of government requirements. This has been the government's unwritten policy since the late 1950s; it became official policy subsequent to being recommended in the final report of the Packard Commission, June 1986.

Types of Contracts

In the 1950s, most contracts awarded were firm-fixed-price contracts. Such contracts were the most difficult to negotiate, as contractors had to include all contingencies in their costs and buyers had to be astute enough to locate and eliminate the excesses. In some instances, when uncertainties were too great, cost-reimbursement contracts were used. For R&D projects, fixed-price redeterminable contracts were awarded, with the price finalized during performance—after approximately 85% of the work was complete. From the 1960s until the present, however, fixed-price incentive contracts have been used extensively for procurement of major systems, and cost-reimbursement contracts for R&D projects.

In some quarters, the government now considers cost-reimbursement contracts the most demanding to negotiate, possibly because of the reliance placed on the Truth in Negotiation Act. Government procurement regulations recommend that fixed-price contracts not be used for any project in which too many unknowns exist. Nevertheless, the fixed-price incentive contract is classified as a fixed-price contract and used extensively on major systems; as projects advance and changes materialize, contractors fail to submit cost data and negotiate the price—until the work is almost complete. The prime beneficiary of such contracts is the system contractor, who could receive an approximately 12% profit rather than the 6-8% it would receive under a cost-reimbursement contract. And the cost to the taxpayer on a billion-dollar project is $40 million to $120 million, with little or no risk to the contractor.

A fixed-price incentive contract is not truly a fixed-price contract; too many variables are involved. To illustrate: At the outset the government buyer and the contractor must negotiate several basic pricing elements—target cost, target profit, target price, ceiling price. (If, for example, the target cost is $10 million and the target profit is $1 million, the ceiling price would be $12 million—usually approximately 20% above the target cost.) The buyer and contractor must also consider the share ratio—the percentages of savings to accrue to the government and to the contractors. Often the award of a major system is initiated simply with a letter contract that cites the type of contract anticipated (fixed price incentive), the dates on which cost data are due and negotiations are to take place, and the dollar amount authorized to be expended by the contractor. This method only encourages numerous changes and delays in the contractor's submission of cost data and negotiation of the price.

Many people—commanding officers, project managers, heads of departments, and administrators, all of whom are outside procurement—have restricted the use of certain types of contracts at the expense of the government. Even though time and material, labor hour, and letter contracts are excellent contractual vehicles for certain situations, they are rarely used, and their absence adds to the government's cost. For example, the use of a time and material contract to cover the repair of air-conditioning equipment when a government engineer is available to monitor the contractor's work would be excellent. With a taboo on the use of a time and material contract, however, a firm-fixed-price contract or cost-reimbursement contract may be awarded. The firm-fixed-price contract would have to be loaded to cover all contingencies (including imaginary ones), and the cost-reimbursement contract might result in the use of higher-priced personnel and more hours to perform the work.

Since the 1950s, then, several major changes have occurred in the process of procurement.

1. The amount of cost information required of large contractors has been limited;

2. The dollar value of contracts and subcontracts has significantly increased;

3. Government procurement dollars are now concentrated in a relatively small number of firms;

4. The qualifications for government buyers have decreased;

5. Methods of costing, auditing, and contract administration have changed, resulting in looser cost control; and

6. The type of contract awarded for major systems has changed.

The result: By the late 1960s, runaway costs had become endemic to government procurement.

3.
Marketing to the Government versus Marketing to the Private Sector

Before considering costs, one needs to discuss the differences between marketing to the government and to the private sector. The word "marketing" is all-encompassing, covering supply, demand, pricing, selling, financing, productive capacity, research and development, advertising, public relations, packaging, and packing. Industries whose major client is the government do not react to the normal market stimuli of supply and demand, and marketing to the government is less expensive than marketing to the private sector.

The ideology expressed in the Federal Acquisition Regulation (FAR) and other government regulations about the treatment of costs, the allowability and allocability of costs, and the profitability of suppliers does not exist in the private sector. For example, Cost Accounting Standard 414, DOD FAR Supplement Part 15.901, and FAR Subpart 15.8, pertaining to the weighted guidelines method of determining profit, all permit an additional factor for "facilities capital cost of money" that is beyond the allowance for depreciation. The purpose of this cost element is to compensate contractors for their capital investment in plants and equipment. No such rigid treatment of cost elements is used in pricing in the private sector, however, because of the competition. Further, the private market contains numerous imponderables—

not present in the government procurement market—that are nevertheless permitted to be offset against government business.

This chapter discusses only seven of the more significant imponderables: independent research and development (company-sponsored); finances; selling expense; treatment of costs; practices involving government-furnished property, government-furnished equipment, leasing, and subcontracting; pricing; and profitability.

IR&D

Some of the reasons for introducing a new commercial item or service must be recognized. Some products are developed to round out a firm's product line, to keep out competition, or to get a foot in the door. In other cases, market research supports a need for the product, or a company wants to introduce a new product to use idle plant capacity. Other companies develop a product simply because the president or board of directors wants it developed. Many of these reasons result in an unprofitable item.

To develop a commercial item for the private sector, a firm has to cover, up front, its total costs, including research and development; the fabrication of prototypes, tools, dies, jigs, and equipment; inventory; market research; advertising; and finance costs. Costs of IR&D for commercial products are an overhead item usually budgeted at the beginning of the fiscal year and are one of the first areas to be curtailed or dropped when business falls off. Industries generally allocate and expend approximately 2% or less of their sales for company-sponsored IR&D. Industrywide, for the past 25 years, under 5% of all new items have proven profitable, but with payments for IR&D from the government, many major government contractors show expenditures for IR&D of

1-5% of sales—or 1-5% of billions of dollars, 50% or more of which are subcontracted.

Today, a major government contractor having non-government sales or attempting to develop a new product to supplement its government business can treat repackaging or developing a commercial item as independent research and development costs that can be allocated, in whole or in part, to its government business. It can take known components, for example, repackage them into a new product, charge it to IR&D, and allocate those expenses to government business. Furthermore, the cost of this IR&D would appear under general and administrative expense in financial statements rather than under manufacturing overhead, engineering overhead, or factory burden, which are all overhead accounts in accordance with generally accepted accounting practices. Although a ceiling has been placed on the amount of IR&D expense a major contractor can recover in any one fiscal period, the government lacks an audit trail and the ceiling therefore is meaningless. The annual cost to taxpayers is approximately $18 billion—over and above what the government continues to sponsor, through contracts, for research and development.

When the government awards major contractors a contract for research and development, the contract is usually in a technical area that the firm might have sponsored on its own. In general, because a firm's capability for R&D is limited, receipt of government sponsorship in a given area means that the firm's research for that product is no longer an indirect or overhead item and that the funds that would otherwise be spent on the research may therefore be diverted to another of the company's activities. Further, the company is entitled to receive reimbursement for part or all of its company-sponsored IR&D.

Finances

The government allows no interest expense to be allocated to its business, primarily because it provides for progress payments that cover most incurred costs under a contract, even though it has not yet received a product. Having received progress payments, major government contractors have billions of dollars of unliquidated progress payments that are offset as deliveries are made. Consequently, government contractors must finance only approximately 20% of their government sales, whereas in sales to the private sector those same contractors must finance 35% to well over 1,000% (in the case of a loss) of their sales.

Often, contractors use contract funds to procure test and production equipment, referred to as "contractor-acquired government property." Capital production equipment procured by the contractor for use under a specific contract is usually depreciated during the life of the contract. In the case of both contractor-acquired government property and capital production equipment procured by the contractor, the government has paid for the equipment while the contractor generally retains it—a situation not likely to happen in the private sector.

Selling Expense

The government simplifies the marketing of many commonly procured items to its agencies. Furthermore, because each agency's sales potential can be readily identified, a sales campaign can be formulated without very costly advertising programs and with using comparatively few personnel. And many suppliers use salaried rather than commissioned salesmen to sell directly to the government. All of these factors mean that the selling expense is considerably less for a government contract than for a commercial contract.

Treatment of Costs

The Cost Accounting Standards and the government's contract cost principles allow major government contractors to disregard generally accepted accounting practices by establishing multiple cost centers to minimize their risks and produce the greatest monetary return. To illustrate: An unrealistic number of cost centers for a contractor means that each center becomes a business unit or subcontractor capable of billing the prime contractor using its own indirect rates (to which the prime contractor's indirect rates are then added)— which generally account for 35-65% of a selling price and which may vary considerably from the prime contractor's rates. Although a particular cost center might be a support group for an entire corporation—technical publications, for example—setting it up as a cost center means that labor costs can be charged directly to the government contract. And that almost invariably means that the government contract will be charged a disproportionate amount of such costs. It also means that most indirect costs in these cost centers could be attributed to the government business, because indirect costs for commercial business are treated quite differently.

On a competitive government procurement, the price arrived at using such a practice would be excessive, and contractors routinely submit bids stating that the contract will be performed by one group and listing the subcontractors. Changing the bid to include subcontractors (inter- and intra-corporate) after the contract is awarded, however, is often done, even though it is contrary to the Cost Accounting Standards and to contract cost principles. And the change is significant, because it affects the indirect rate structures of all the groups involved. The regulations do not cite any specific penalties for such actions, and government personnel usually ignore the issue in favor of getting the job done expeditiously and retaining the good will and support of their superiors and the contractor.

Further, when contractors are contemplating such changes, they are required to submit a cost impact statement showing any change in costs for their government contracts that would result from the new practice; they are also required to negotiate any resulting changes in price with the contracting officer. Contractors and government personnel alike, however, have ignored the requirement for cost impact statements.

Government-Furnished Property; Government-Furnished Equipment; Leasing and/or Subcontracting

Prime contractors receive another break in their government contracts that is not available for vendors to the private sector. The government often furnishes property (GFP) or equipment (GFE) or allows the contractor to subcontract or lease the required facilities and equipment. Even though such breaks can be worth hundreds of millions of dollars, no guidance is available on their costing. Furthermore, GFP and GFE are not taken into consideration when profit rates are determined; nor are they always addressed during negotiations.

Pricing

Pricing products and services for commercial customers often depends greatly on factors other than actual costs—competition, the nature of the product, potential customers, potential for marketing, inventory, and current plant use, for example. Many items must be underpriced to sell; others are priced at whatever the market will bear, encouraging imitations and eventually leading to reduced prices.

The government is often overcharged for commercial products for several reasons: different methods of distribution; lack of quantity discounts; and the considerably lower selling, administrative, finance costs, and the types of industries that are associated with government sales.

Methods of Distribution. The pricing of a commercial product must take into account the channels of distribution. Are distributors, wholesalers, agents, or retailers to be involved? Establishing whether they are is essential for determining the financing and marketing staff required for a given product. A manufacturer often sells its products directly to the government, completely omitting from the picture the retailer and its 30% markup. Further, although a manufacturer may usually employ commissioned salesmen in selling commercial customers, in marketing products to the government, it often employs trainees or others on a straight salary, at considerably less cost. On other than commercial products, commissions are included in overhead or another indirect cost element, which for government contracting is an allowable expense. Accordingly, manufacturers receive a double cost benefit when they bid on other than commercial items for the government.

Quantity Discounts. Although the U.S. government is the biggest purchaser of goods and services in the world, it has not been accorded the best prices across the board, because the manner in which funds are appropriated, prevents the government from placing a single order, since appropriations are made to each agency and consolidation of all needs is impractical. The Federal Supply Schedule (FSS) contracts, awarded to facilitate the procurement of commercially available goods and services required by various government agencies, cite the goods and/or services offered, contractor, term of contract, price, terms, conditions, and so on. After the government and the contractors notify the agencies about the FSS contracts awarded, the agencies can issue delivery orders against the FSS contract, price, terms, and conditions that have been agreed to. Each delivery order cites the individual agencies funding authorization. Both the government's task of securing many items and industries' marketing are simplified. Nothing comparable exists outside the government.

The cost of manufacturing generally decreases as the production run increases. A manufacturer takes into consideration anticipated sales to the government in forecasting production, and the expected production of large quantities affects the commercial pricing structure for a given product. In general, pricing major cost items is based on accumulating all engineering, design, tooling, set-up, and marketing costs, prorating them over a specified number of units, and then adding the manufacturing cost to each unit. If the number of units sold is fewer than anticipated, the firm can lose money; if, however, more units are sold than anticipated, the firm can receive windfall profits. The government should not be denied the best price when it is a supplier's largest customer.

Selling, Administrative, and Finance Costs for Government Sales. A firm requires less private financing for its government business, and it takes less risk with regard to delinquent payments and bad debts, because the firm can sell to the government without having a salesman on the payroll and because it often receives progress payments for items requiring long lead time. These practices are seldom found in the private sector; their absence adds to the administrative cost of commercial sales. The government should not have to pay the same high costs the private sector does.

Types of Industries. In specifying requirements for pricing, the government recognizes four basic types of industries: services, manufacturing (specification requirements), research and development, and construction. Each category entails a significantly different structure for costing, which may vary from industry to industry and from company to company within an industry.

• *Services.* For a bidder, the price of services depends on several factors—the nature of the service, the type of personnel involved, where the service is to be performed in relation to the home office or plant, and the nature and extent of backup support. Because of the nature of the equipment manufactured, a contractor might be compelled to offer the requested services at cost or below—or be faced with the prospect of a competitor's servicing its equipment. In many companies, a service group is part of a larger group, and the rate structure is based on the larger group's rate structure. In such firms, rates and other costs quoted for services are likely to be on the high side. When the service group is a separate entity, rates quoted are apt to be more reasonable.

• *Manufacturing (specification requirements).* Most government procurements involve sole-source, negotiated contracts. The lack of competition decreases the customer's knowledge of the supplier's costs and increases the government's price.

• *R&D.* When the government awards a cost-reimbursement R&D contract, it accepts all incurred costs up to a cited dollar limitation. It also permits its suppliers to charge the government for their company-sponsored projects, whether or not they are truly R&D projects and whether or not they apply to the government's requirements.

• *Construction.* Construction contracts tend to be firm-fixed-price contracts, but changes are inevitable and the manner in which contractors are requested to break out costs is therefore of paramount importance. Because construction contracts are often advertised, firm-fixed-price awards, the general tendency has been to disregard any breakout of the various aspects of the project for pricing, with the result that when modifications to the original plans are required, basic costing data to compute the cost of the changes are lacking.

Even though a large corporation can include all four

types of industries, the government should not allow a major manufacturer to break out its costs as if they were composed of 20 to 40 separate operations, because all the operations are likely to support the firm's major capability. Breaking out costs in that way makes the costs impossible to audit and the resultant rates more vulnerable to fluctuation; and subjecting each of the 20 to 40 segments to separate indirect rates usually increases the cost to the government.

Profitability

Management is responsible for producing a reasonable, plausible profit. But the government's practice of permitting costs for nongovernment sales to be offset against government business allows the profitability of government sales to be greatly distorted.

This was quite evident when a conglomerate acquired a very profitable government contractor and the contractor's profitability then disappeared—a disappearance directly attributable to the allowability and allocability of costs. All too often the outcome for a product line, a plant, or a division is presented in financial statements as a loss attributable to a firm's government rather than its commercial business. Thus, industry maintains that its commercial sales are more profitable than its government business, and several profit study reports sponsored by DOD and the General Accounting Office (GAO) support industry's claim. (However, the most recent report, by GAO, disputes that claim.) All the reports are badly flawed in that inadequate or no consideration is given to government financing in the form of progress payments, government-furnished equipment, government-furnished facilities (plant and equipment), and contractor-acquired equipment and property. When government business represents even 5-10% of a large corporation's sales, those sales generally represent far more than 5-10% of pro-fits. Even when a firm bids a defense contract at a loss, it is often able either to reduce the amount of a known or anticipated loss or to turn a loss into a profit. For example, a contractor might knowingly have part or all of a plant idle. Taking a defense contract at an unrealistically low price or moving a government project from another facility to it might benefit the contractor by covering part of its fixed overhead costs and thereby reducing the dollar amount of the loss. In most cases involving large corporations, losses are turned into profitable situations at the government's expense.

Nonetheless, industry officials claim they do not want government business—thus securing government business on their own terms and, in the process, leaving the impression that they are doing the government a favor. Although some company officials have said they will not undertake any government business at a loss, many of their firms consistently lose money on commercial business and could not survive without the government's business. Without the government's business, who would buy the sophisticated weaponry the companies produce? And where would they find another multibillion dollar product to replace the military products they produce?

With a sound base for its business in the form of a sizable government contract, management enjoys ample room to maneuver with respect to the balance of its business. The large government contract also permits a significant portion of a company's overhead on commercial business to be absorbed by the government (which significantly increases the cost to the government).

4.
Costs

Most articles dealing with the elimination of cost overruns concentrate on systems procurement, program management, efficiency, economy, fraud, abuse, or waste. Although concentrating on these areas might result in savings, they are areas that government users and engineers—not procurement personnel—should address.

And although the nation is concerned about cost overruns and cost growth on major government contracts, the most that is said about "costs" in the most recent commission report, the Packard Commission report, is the need for contractors' self-governance in that area. Self-governance has not worked in the past, however, and it is unlikely to work in the future.

The fact remains that the government can save approximately 15%—or $30 billion—annually simply by incorporating improvements in the procurement area. Most of them would be in costing and could be implemented immediately, without any new legislation or regulations.

Furthermore, Cost Accounting Standards and DCAA's and DLA's guidelines and practices, instead of assisting government procurement personnel to establish a "reasonable" price for goods and services, are a barrier to the buyer who seeks meaningful cost data and reasonable prices. Seldom is the true condition of a contractor's accounting system and records apparent; many of those records cannot be audited. Nevertheless, firms are continually awarded contracts totaling billions of dollars. Why? Who is responsible?

The regulations and procedures put in place since the early 1960s have been restrictive, ignoring generally accepted business and accounting practices for negotiation. Consequently, under the present system, no way exists to monitor or audit major government contractors' costs, because the government does not have access to all the necessary cost data. And numerous questions remain unanswered: At what point is a sale complete under a completed contract method of accounting? At what point does a contractor record a sale and related costs for an unpriced contract modification or for a cost-plus-fixed-fee contract? What price is charged for material under a "last-in-first-out" inventory system, when it takes five to ten years to complete a contract? All these factors significantly affect a contractor's rate structure and final price to the government.

The major losers as a result of the erroneous picture painted of a firm's profitability are its customers and investors. When all essential factors are properly considered, a firm's commercial business is seldom more profitable than its government business. For example, many government contractors in the 1970s claimed overruns against the government ranging from $100 million to more than $1 billion, but those overruns seldom appeared in the firms' annual reports or its reports to the Securities and Exchange Commission. Consequently, the Renegotiation Board seldom considered a government contractor's claims in its deliberations, because its deliberations were generally tied to the firm's federal income tax return. The same scenario concerning the profitability of major government contractors is prevalent today.

Seldom do government auditors receive sufficient information about costs to make a reasoned judgment for the treatment and allocation of costs—simply because they see only excerpts of a firm's financial statement. The government has taken the position that it is not concerned with how a contractor handles its government fixed-price or nongovernment business. But these areas are the ones where most abuses occur, enabling a contractor to allocate costs for its commercial business to its government contracts.

Under present industry and government practices and guidelines, many variables and constraints make it impossible to track and control the costs charged to a program. The final cost is usually what management wants it to be, not what it actually is. Firms that have been paid millions of dollars by the government to computerize their cost systems to report program costs accurately have not done so. The treatment of certain corporate costs—home office expense, independent research and development, warranties, and interest, for example—in many instances is so distorted that the true cost of a firm's government product is compromised before the item is even produced. "Pooled" or indirect costs, many of them transferred from a firm's commercial activity to its government business, are not audited by government personnel. And abuses in the treatment of costs have been encouraged by the differential treatment of costs for firm-fixed-price and cost-plus-fixed-fee contracts and by DCAA's interpretation and implementation of regulations.

The treatment of costs is different for each of four groups: the Internal Revenue Service, government contracts, the Renegotiation Board (now defunct), and commercial business.

• IRS is interested only in a firm's profit and loss reported after total income, costs, and expenses are treated in accordance with generally accepted accounting practices and the tax code. Accordingly, IRS does not concern itself with the allowability and allocability of costs under the government's contract cost principles and regulations.

One section of the IRS tax code, however, can significantly affect a firm's reported income, expenses, and profit and loss for its domestic operations. That section deals with the establishment of foreign sales corporations by U.S. corporations. The purpose of the section is to encourage domestic companies to export goods and services by permitting the domestic corporation to sell its goods to a foreign sales corporation at an arbitrary or artificial price (at cost or below) and by exempting 15% of the foreign sales corporation's profit from federal income tax. Such foreign corporations have a definite impact on a firm's reported profit and loss and thus on its federal income tax return. Consequently, how the parent corporation segregates and allocates the costs of sales to a foreign sales corporation can affect the firm's government contract costs.

- The pricing, treatment, and allocation of costs and expenses for a contractor's government business are generally significantly different from those for its commerical business. Further complicating the issue is that the government permits a significantly different treatment of costs for fixed-price and for cost-reimbursement contracts, resulting in multiple cost centers and associated rates for each.

- The Renegotiation Board generally permitted government contractors to use a sales ratio for the allocation of costs to their government and nongovernment business.[3] This practice had a twofold effect: (1) It offset any excessive profit on a single contract or between a firm's commercial and government business because renegotiation was based on total government business in any one fiscal period, not on each contract; and (2) it ignored the contractor's costing practices for its government business. Furthermore, renegotiation was

---

3. A more detailed presentation of the process of renegotiation appears in chapter 7.

tied to the contractor's federal income tax return. Many of the major contractors who claimed significant overruns against the government reported few if any of those claims in their federal income tax returns, and most claims were therefore not reviewed. And—because those claims were paid but not reported—what action did the auditors take to recompute, for each fiscal period involved, the indirect rates, which were undoubtedly affected? All indications are that it was an impossible task and that the rates were not recomputed.

• Even though a contractor's costs on its commercial business may affect its costs on government business, the possibility of government auditors' examining those costs is nil. Furthermore, neither costs for a firm-fixed-price contract nor costs on a firm's commercial business are subject to audit, even though they may affect a firm's indirect costs.

• As long as a contractor's accounting system is based on generally accepted accounting practices and deviations are made in compliance with government regulations, the government accepts it. Although the contractor is required to adhere to certain requirements for allowability of costs—interest and entertainment are not allowable, for example—and to the treatment and allocation of costs in general, the government does not attempt to impose any particular accounting system on a contractor.

Major government contractors' treatment of costs, in accordance with government regulations, is overly complex and restrictive and should be simplified. The treatment of costs for government contracts ignores the treatment accorded for fixed-price and nongovernment business and for industrywide pricing practices, all of which are very flexible. Furthermore, a disparity exists between the treatment of costs for government cost-reimbursement contracts and for firm-fixed-price contracts.

It is because of this nonstandard treatment of costs for

different types of government contracts that small business often cannot compete with large corporations. A firm with no risk, operating primarily under cost-reimbursement government contracts, receives an added bonus: It can usually quote a much lower rate for overhead and general and administrative (G&A) expense than can a firm performing mostly under firm-fixed-price contracts. The contractor's efficiency or technical competency does not enter the picture. This quirk makes the government responsible for unfair competition through the bidding process.

Theoretically, the total costs under a fixed-price and a cost-reimbursement contract would be about the same. In reality, however, that equivalence is undermined by the business environment and the mechanics established for bidding on government and nongovernment requirements. Table 4 shows how bids for the same requirement might look for two firms, one having primarily cost-reimbursement contracts and the other firm-fixed-price contracts.

TABLE 4

Impact of Rate Structure on Bidding Process— Fixed Price versus Cost Reimbursement

	Company A Cost-Plus-Fixed-Fee Contract	Company B Fixed-Price Contract
Material	$100	$ 100
Labor[a]	400	300
O.H. (50% of direct labor)	200	
O.H. (150% of direct labor)		450
	$700	$ 850
G&A (12%)	84	
G&A (15%)		128
	$784	$ 978
Profit (8%)	63	78
Selling Price	$847	$1,056

[a] The difference between companies A and B results from the treatment accorded certain costs; for example, testing, laboratory, and report writing personnel would be charged to "direct labor" in cost-plus-fixed-fee contracts and to "indirect labor" for fixed-price contracts.

A case that more vividly illustrates the point involves the same two firms' bidding a task on a fixed-price, level-of-effort basis in which the customer wants a technical area investigated—a task that requires the services of two senior physicists for a year. With the two firms using the same overhead and G&A rates as in the previous table and assuming that a senior physicist receives $50,000 a year, the quotations would be as shown in table 5.

TABLE 5

Impact of Rate Structure on Bidding
Research and Development (Services) Efforts

	Company A Cost-Plus-Fixed- Fee Contract	Company B Fixed-Price Contract
Direct labor (two senior physicists @ $50,000 per year)	$100,000	$100,000
Overhead (50% of direct labor)	50,000	
Overhead (150% of direct labor)		150,000
	$150,000	$250,000
G&A (12%)	18,000	
G&A (15%)		37,500
	$168,000	$287,500
Profit (8%)	13,440	23,000
Selling Price	$181,440	$310,500

Table 5 focuses attention on the impact that the government's costing principles, regulations, and practices have on the bidding process. Contractors are encouraged to charge as much as possible to direct costs in cost-reimbursement contracts, whereas contractors bidding on a fixed-price contract use generally accepted accounting practices. Accordingly, the "pools" for the firm predominantly oriented toward fixed-price contracts might include costs for travel, testing, and secretarial services, whereas those same costs might be treated as direct costs for a cost-reimbursement contract—a decided advantage for the firm primarily performing under cost-reimbursement contracts!

This practice is further aggravated by the practice of government auditors' treating identical costs differently in different parts of the country.

The preceding discussion highlights some of the areas that (1) make the government's current contract costing practices almost impossible to audit, (2) allow the government to be billed for costs that are not applicable to its contracts, and (3) are responsible for creating unfair competition during bidding. A significant amount of money can be saved by (1) simplifying the accounting treatment accorded costs for government contracts, (2) adhering to generally accepted accounting and business practices, and (3) requiring major government contractors to submit their latest financial statements with their cost proposals. Major companies should be treated no differently from small companies with respect to submitting cost data.

If significant improvements are to be made in the price the government pays for goods and services, the area of cost data must be given top priority. Congress is ignoring the issue, however, and is passing statutes, such as appropriation bills, with sections covering the treatment of costs that were disallowed or cut back in the 1950s and that since then have been allowed by auditors and other government personnel. Recently implemented is an unorthodox computation for profit—a computation in which G&A expense is excluded in arriving at the profit rate, for example. This nonstandard treatment of costs can only compound an already bad situation. The areas most worthy of simplification and clarification, however—the treatment of costs for government contracts and the financial information contractors must furnish government personnel—should be clearly specified in legislation to preclude any misunderstanding or legal recourse.

Table 3 (see chapter 2), although admittedly oversimplifying the treatment accorded cost elements in the 1950s and in the mid-1980s, highlights the cost elements that a contractor can adjust in preparing a bid for the government's requirements. The following discussion of cost elements may shed some light on current practices during negotiations for goods and services.

Material

"Materials" include subcontracting, spare parts, parts used in the fabrication of equipment, and raw material. Also included but not always broken out are tools, dies, jigs, and special test and production equipment.

Because of IRS regulations and government procurement regulations, the treatment accorded costs of material for accounting raises many questions. Under certain conditions and for tax purposes, a contractor can change its method of costing material during a contract period from first-in-first-out to last-in-first-out or vice versa. The change generally is for the purpose of permitting the contractor to use the most costly material in its inventory first. As government contractors incur charges for material, however they usually receive progress payments of approximately 80%. Although one might assume that the cost charged would be the cost as of the date the material was billed the government, that might not be the case, especially on programs extending over three, five, or ten years. Sheet steel used for shipbuilding, for example, might have been tossed into a kitty and buried and the government subsequently billed at a higher price than the contractor actually incurred.

Materials for the maintenance and repair of plant production equipment and for travel, quality control, and inspection can be listed as a direct charge on government contracts but are seldom treated that way for nongovernment business. Therefore, they should never be permitted to be listed as a direct charge on government contracts, because to do so means that the government picks up a share of the contractor's nongovernment expenses and is therefore precluded from auditing those costs.

Subcontracting/Materials Handling. Subcontracting, as discussed in this book, is intended to be all-inclusive and applies to raw material, parts, and subcontracting, including consultants, research and development programs, and any other efforts procured by the prime contractor from other sources. In government contracting, however, subcontracting has a much narrower connotation and refers to systems and subsystems that for the most part operate independently and to which the prime contractor adds little, if anything; an aircraft engine would be an example of such a system or subsystem.

As a result of the government's implementing the concept of systems procurement, the cost of subcontracting went from approximately 30% of the selling price in the 1950s to a range of 50–70% today. The prime contractor is reimbursed for all effort (labor, overhead, and so on) expended in securing the subcontracted items, but what factor should the contractor add to the price of subcontracted goods and services and other material costs? Some contractors levy a materials handling or service charge that might range from 1–15% for administration of subcontracts and other material costs. Others do not have such a pool. In either event, material costs including material handling costs are subject to the G&A expense, which might range from 25–35% and a profit of 10–12% is added to the sum of subcontracting, material handling or service charge, and G&A expense. When costs for subcontracts represent hundreds of millions of dollars, the added charges represent an exorbitant price for the government to pay a middle man for placing an order. Further, application of the government's weighted guidelines for determining profit permits the contractor to secure added consideration for its subcontracting (in the narrower sense) by permitting a higher weighting factor, because the government considers the contractor to be exposed to a greater risk in subcontracting than if it were to produce the item in-house. In R&D, where funding is limited, this extra consideration is also a factor. Subcontracting is a major contributor to cost overruns and cost growth on major programs.

Parts/Spare Parts. For government-specified items and high-cost industry-developed items, the government generally requires the manufacturer to submit a bill of materials in two sections. One covers commercially available parts, indicating the manufacturer, part number, stock number, and quantity required per unit; the other requires the same information for nonstandard parts and asemblies. Industry in general, however, has refused to supply the government with a list of common, off-the-shelf items. And this "oversight" is not insignificant. If a common washer were replaced by one made of the wrong metal or the wrong dimensions or were lubricated with the wrong lubricant, it could wreak havoc in a multimillion dollar system, and so it is therefore imperative that the government know precisely who manufactured the original components. And with the significant increase in the dollar value of subcontracting under systems procurement, the procurement of spare parts becomes critical.

In the 1950s, the Air Force would appropriate funds, generally ranging from 25–40% of the value of the end item, for spare parts at the time it awarded a contract. Under that procedure, the obligated funds were in escrow for several years. When funds were urgently needed in the 1960s, that hoard was raided—and it has never been restored. Allowing contractors to receive the full amount of indirect costs plus profit for spare parts, major components, and replacement equipment for which they place an order is granting them a windfall in income.

Raw Material. In the prime contractor's invoices, this cost element, in systems procurement, is drastically understated because of the significant amount of "value added" to raw material by first-, second-, third-, and fourth-tier subcontractors. Rather, subcontract costs are recorded as purchased parts or subcontracts on the prime contractor's invoices.

Material at Standard Cost. Many contractors use a standard cost system that cites material as a certain cost per unit. Generally, neither the contractor's cost breakdown nor the DCAA audit report explains what the cost per unit covers (it would cover costs of materials, rejects, and spoilage). The standard cost of materials for government jobs generally results in a favorable variance that invariably disappears when costs are allocated between government and nongovernment business.

Often included under "material" are tools, jigs, dies, and special test and production equipment. In fact, however, they are capital expenditures, which means they should be capitalized and written off in some fashion—per unit, for example—or amortized over a period of years. But too often the cost of such items is written off in the period in which it was incurred. Expenditures for special test and production equipment (contractor-acquired government property) are also usually written off in the period in which the cost is incurred, and contractors invariably receive a profit on such expenditures. Granting contractors a profit on such equipment purchases should be prohibited.

Direct Labor

Direct labor is labor that can readily be identified with one cost objective, such as a project or a contract.

The treatment accorded costs for direct labor depends

upon many factors—the nature of the contractor's business, the contractor's accounting system, the type of contract (cost reimbursement or firm fixed price), and the number of the contractor's employees—which in turn affect indirect costs like overhead and G&A expenses. Accordingly, the more direct labor that can be charged, the more competitive the contractor's indirect rates, because overhead is generally expressed as a percentage of indirect manufacturing costs (overhead) to direct labor. Approximately 20 different bases are used to allocate overhead, depending upon the nature of the contractor's business.

Officers' compensation, in accordance with generally accepted accounting principles, is treated as indirect labor and appears as G&A expense. For the government, however, if an officer's salary can be attributed to a cost objective (a contract), it should be moved from indirect labor to direct labor. In that event, the contractor receives three competitive advantages: (1) Its overhead rate decreases; (2) its G&A expense is also reduced; and (3) the contractor experiences less risk. Encouraging contractors to treat as direct charges as many costs as possible guarantees overruns on subsequent contracts, because many of the costs continue after the government contract concludes and are then treated as indirect costs.

Direct labor is probably the highest-risk cost element confronting any firm, commercial or government—oriented. The higher the payroll costs in relation to sales, the more readily a profit can be turned into a loss by the retention of the labor force beyond the period of its full productivity. Further, the government's requirements have created a specialized labor force that may need retraining in new fields or current technologies in the event of securing a new project or a layoff; thus, the risk for the government, the contractor, and its employees is great, whereas a firm manufacturing for the private sector has an incentive to reduce its labor force when business falls off. The same incentives and opportunities for reemployment are not necessarily available in the government sector.

Figure 1 depicts the technical and production labor force of a prime contractor during the life of a program.

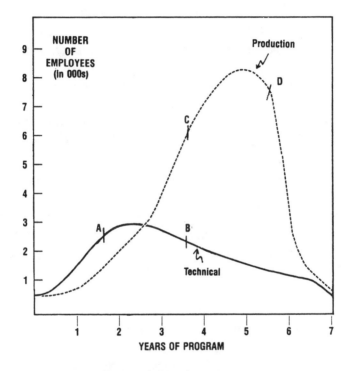

FIGURE 1
Technical and Production Labor Force
Required during a Program

Between points A and B, and C and D, the contractor should start bidding on new programs in anticipation of the immediate project's ending. New major government projects are scarce and unpredictable, however, and the following factors work against a contractor's reducing the work force for a government project:

• The posssibility of having a facility with no work and no employees—a prime consideration in not adhering to an established delivery schedule, especially an unrealistic one;

• The difficulty of replacing the specialized labor force;

• The need to have employees propose and quote new programs to the government;

• The anticipation of engineering changes in the existing system;

• Reduced profits on in-house programs.

In retaining surplus labor on government programs, contractors are confronted with leaving the employees in existing direct labor categories, a procedure that the government could criticize as inefficient and wasteful, or transferring them to indirect labor categories. Contractors frequently choose the latter option, which results in a significant increase in overhead. Some of these employees are assigned to company-sponsored projects, and the government bears the bulk of the costs under expenses for IR&D. Although one might question a firm's right to reclassify labor categories or to switch workers to different cost elements, the option nevertheless rests entirely with the contractor. It is this area that prompts some government personnel to say industry is inefficient, but under present statutes and regulations, industry would be penalizing itself by releasing its labor force in a timely manner. To compound the problem, the talents of a contractor's surplus labor force may not be adequate for the government's current projects.

Under existing government statutes and regulations,

• The government does not have the right to disallow labor costs. A government buyer might deem the hourly rate excessive, but if that rate is the rate a contractor pays its employees, the government has no recourse.

• If the auditor finds the number of hours quoted excessive, the government negotiator is responsible for reducing costs in negotiations by reducing the number of hours.

• The government may determine that certain direct labor should be treated as indirect labor, and vice versa, resulting in a dispute between government and the contractor.

• Nothing currently prevents a contractor from understating its indirect expense rates for bidding purposes.

Overall direct labor costs as a percentage of total procurement dollars expended have decreased by approximately 60% since the 1950s. This situation is directly attributable to the significant increase in subcontracting and to the accompanying increase in billings for indirect costs and profit.

Fringe Benefits

Fringe benefits include health insurance, social security payments, life insuarnce, sick leave, annual leave, education and training, bonuses, and pensions. In the 1950s, they amounted to approximately 5-15% of labor costs; today, they account for from 25% to over 50% of labor dollars. For government contractors three costs—insurance, bonuses (including stock option plans), and pensions—often equal or exceed the fringe benefits that government employees receive. Most distressing is the treatment accorded bonuses. For some contractors, bonuses amount to 20% or more of labor costs and are in reality a distribution of profits but are not treated as such for tax purposes.[4] And even though industry's management and technical performance for most major government projects have been less than outstanding and bonuses

---

4. The IRS is not concerned about bonuses as a distribution of profit, because it will receive income taxes either from the individuals to whom the bonus was given or from the company.

have still been awarded, DCAA, DCASMA, and procurement personnel have refused to take a stand on the subject. Once paid, bonuses are included in the expense pool used to compute the fringe benefit or other indirect rate, thereby guaranteeing it forever after. The government should not permit bonuses to be included in the computation of indirect rates, even if they are covered by a labor contract. And Congress should put a ceiling on the fringe benefits allowed.

Currently there are no firm guidelines concerning the treatment of fringe benefits. Nevertheless, from a cost standpoint, it does make a difference as to whether they are included in direct labor or are a separate add-on cost factor.

Bidding and Billing Direct Labor and Fringe Benefits

No guidance currently exists for the treatment of direct labor and fringe benefits, and consequently their treatment is not uniform. DCAA audit reports seldom contain supporting cost schedules for fringe benefits. Fringe benefits are a significant portion of labor costs, and how they are presented affects price. Detailed guidance for their treatment should be available, but neither the FAR, contract cost principles, or Cost Accounting Standards covers the subject.

Indirect Costs

Indirect costs—costs that cannot be readily identified with a cost objective like a contract or a project—include materials handling, engineering overhead, manufacturing overhead, G&A expense, and the costs of developing bids and proposals (B&P) and independent research and development (IR&D). Combined, these indirect expenses represent approximately 35–65% of the selling price of all goods and services sold to the government. Regulations require that a contractor have supporting schedules for both the base and the expense pool used to compute each indirect rate (expressed as a percent) used in the preparation of cost proposals and billings to the government.

Most major government contractors have three to thirty cost centers, each with a different set of indirect expense rates. For each cost center, in each fiscal year, auditors must review and negotiate four sets of rates:

• *Actual or final rates*—based on actual costs and used to close out cost-reimbursement and incentive contracts.

• *Interim billing rates*—used in determining progress payments and payments under cost-reimbursement contracts.

• *Bidding rates*—used in bidding new jobs and based on estimated costs.

• *Advance bidding rates*—projections of indirect expense rates used in quoting long-term contracts.

Nothing prevents a contractor from understating its bidding rates and advance bidding rates. To perform their job correctly, government auditors would have to examine a firm's direct and indirect costs to arrive at each of these four sets of rates, multiplied by the number of cost centers involved.

Generally, a contractor submits a proposal for indirect expenses to the government audit group, which results in a review of the contractor's accounting records. But because of the effect of indirect rates on a firm's competitiveness in bidding new business, costs are reclassified constantly throughout a fiscal year, contrary to rules and regulations. In many cases, government personnel are advised after the fact or discover the change during an audit or cost review.

Expenses for travel, quality assurance, and inspection for a firm's nongovernment business are usually treated as indirect expenses, in accordance with generally accepted accounting practices. For government contracts, these expenses can be treated as direct or indirect, amounting to a double charge: The government not only reimburses a contractor for these costs as direct charges, but it also assumes a share of these costs that are charged as indirect for the contractor's nongovernment business. And the government is precluded by regulations and practices from reviewing these costs.

Government regulations also state that a cost, to be allowable and therefore allocable to a government contract, must be "reasonable." Too often, the major government contractors do not supply the cost information required to make that determination for indirect costs. Procurement personnel, moreover, are at the mercy of DCAA, which establishes its own priorities and policies—policies that do not always adhere to the Cost Accounting Standards or contract cost principles promulgated by the CASB or the FAR.

How does an auditor know, for example, that costs for telephone, electricity, depreciation, and other items, each allocated on a different basis, are proper when the entire cost for each is seldom seen by government personnel? The matter is further complicated when a contractor moves nongovernment business into facilities devoted entirely to government contracts and the costs for B&P and IR&D are subsequently transferred from divisions performing nongovernment business to the contractor's government business. DCAA audit reports today seldom address unreasonable costs but present questioned, unsupported, and disallowed costs. And when costs are questioned, unsupported, and/or disallowed, audit reports often set aside the entire cost proposed rather than the amounts in contention.

Although this practice makes it appear that auditors are doing their job well, in reality they are not. In most instances, the amounts set aside are not adequately explained and are therefore of little use to buyers in negotiating a contract or settling a claim. In other instances, because auditors should have access to the contractor's accounting records to support their claims, unsupported and questioned costs raise a serious question about the adequacy of the supplier's accounting system. And lack of complete cost data makes it difficult for government buyers and auditors to make rational decisions about a proposal.

Material Handling/Service Charge. Although material handling or service charge is an important factor when subcontracting and other material costs is a major portion of a contract, in some cases it is negotiated outside of the realm of indirect rates, since contractors do not have formal accounting systems for recording and accumulating costs associated with this function. In other cases, the subcontracting can be considerably greater than anticipated, and a rate is negotiated that is unrealistic. In still other cases, an indirect rate is agreed to without necessary supporting cost schedules. Accordingly, the area needs formal guidelines.

Overhead. Also referred to as burden, manufacturing overhead, engineering overhead, or factory burden, overhead covers those business costs that cannot be readily identified with a contract or a project. In the 1950s, overhead generally covered a firm's expenditures for product improvement and for research and development of new items, as well as the preparation of proposals (because technical personnel were involved). Often the cost was divided into manufacturing overhead and engineering overhead, and firms were very conscious of the effect of those costs on their rate structure and on their ability to be competitive.

Today, many small government contractors still reflect such costs in manufacturing overhead accounts. Major government contractors found, however, that with the implementation of systems procurement, bidding costs were getting out of control and overhead and other indirect costs had to be reported at reasonable rates. Accordingly, the government implemented the concept of including the costs of bidding. R&D, and product improvement in G&A expense, to be treated as a cost objective and recovered in G&A. These costs did not go away; they were simply given new titles and placed in an area where they would have the greatest additional impact on total cost—G&A expense.

The general consensus among government personnel appears to be that the lower the indirect rates, the cheaper the cost to the government. But that assumption does not necessarily hold true. For example, if every cost element of a business were treated as a direct charge, a costly computerized cost accounting system would be required, and indirect rates would be zero. A contractor would readily be able to insert an overhead charge of 25%, however, which, despite its extremely reasonable appearance, would be a double charge.

In the 1950s, firms accumulated R&D costs without reporting them until management decided to write them off as a loss or to capitalize all incurred expenditures, writing them off over a period of time on the basis of cost per unit or cost per year. Today, such costs are generally written off in the year in which they are incurred. Further, the government has furnished plant, equipment, and systems hardware to its contractors, enabling many to maintain an advantage over their competitors in the commercial marketplace.

What base is to be used for the allocation of overhead expense to each cost objective? The most common method of allocating overhead for government contracts is in terms of the direct labor dollar base:

$$\frac{\text{O.H. Expense}}{\text{Direct Labor Dollars (base)}} = \text{O.H. Rate (\%)}$$

Overhead can also be computed a number of other ways:

$$\frac{\text{O.H. Expense}}{\text{Machine Hours}} = \$ \text{ per hour}$$

$$\frac{\text{O.H. Expense}}{\text{Direct Labor Hours}} = \$ \text{ per hour}$$

$$\frac{\text{Indirect Labor Dollars}}{\text{Direct Labor Dollars}}$$

$$\frac{\text{Overhead}}{\text{Direct Material Cost}}$$

$$\frac{\text{Overhead}}{\text{Number of Units Produced}}$$

$$\frac{\text{Total Overhead for Plant}}{\text{Total Hours, Dollars, or Units}}$$

$$\frac{\text{Departmental Direct Labor plus Overhead}}{\text{Departmental Hours, Dollars, or Units}}$$

$$\frac{\text{Overhead}}{\text{Standard Direct Labor Dollars}}$$

$$\frac{\text{Overhead}}{\text{Standard Direct Labor Hours}}$$

$$\frac{\text{Overhead}}{\text{Standard Machine Hours}}$$

Whatever method is chosen, the contractor must be able to support it with schedules for both the expense pool and the base.

General and Administrative Expense. Included in G&A are those expenses incurred by or allocated to a business unit for the management and administration of the entity. Costs included in this category differ from company to company but, in general, they include officers' compensation (including salaries, expenses, bonuses, automobiles, and so on); administrative salaries and wages for clerks, typists, receptionists, secretaries, accountants, bookkeepers, telephone operations, purchasing agents, and contract negotiators and administrators; interest; bad debts; janitorial services; office supplies; utilities; postage; insurance; telephone expenses; stationery and printing; depreciation of office equipment; and maintenance. In addition, many selling expenses are classified under G&A expense. And for government contracts, G&A includes the costs and expenses associated with the preparation of bids and proposals and with independent research and development, although, in accordance with generally accepted accounting practices, such costs are not ordinarily included in G&A. Furthermore, the government's method of charging and allocating G&A expense to government contracts is also not in accordance with generally accepted accounting practices. G&A expense has become a catch-all for various costs, distorting them.

In the 1950s, if significant subcontracting and purchases of material were involved in a contract, the buyer would determine the administrative and managerial effort and expense involved, assess a service or materials handling charge, and establish a rate commensurate with the anticipated administrative cost and a reasonable profit on all those costs. Today, those steps are not likely to take place because of the actions of the contractors, the CASB, DCAA, and the Defense Logistics Agency and because of the very limited role played by procurement personnel in acquisition.

With the establishment of DCAA in 1965 and the Defense Supply Agency (DSA) in 1964, procurement offices turned over a significant portion of their authority and responsibilities to those groups. No longer did procuring departments or agencies dictate policies, practices, and priorities. Most costly to the government was the discarding of the cost analysis function with the introduction of DCAA, and DCAA's manner of auditing costs, and its allocation and treatment of G&A and other indirect costs. From the 1950s until September 1976, contractors were allowed to allocate G&A on the basis of cost of goods sold, which covered material, direct labor, and overhead and which could be allocated between government and nongovernment business on any basis selected. In July 1973, the CASB promulgated Cost Accounting Standard (CAS) 403, "Allocation of Home Office Expenses to Segments," which states that home office expenses should be allocated according to the beneficial or causal relationship between such expenses and the receiving segments. CAS 403 authorized major government contractors to list as direct charges those G&A home office expenses that were identified with specific cost objectives within divisions or subsidiaries. Those expenses that could be identified with two or more corporate segments (entities) or cost objectives of divisions or subsidiaries would be allocated only to those activities on some equitable basis, and the remaining G&A expenses for corporate headquarters would be allocated to all corporate segments on some equitable basis.

On October 1, 1976, CAS 410, "Allocation of Business Unit General and Administrative Expenses to Final Cost Objectives," was implemented. CAS 410 stresses the allocation of G&A expense on the basis of cost input and cites three methods of allocation: (1) total cost input (the preferred method), which would include all identified costs associated with a cost objective incurred in a fiscal year in the base, not just elements included in cost of goods sold; (2) value-added cost input (total cost input less materials and subcontracting), which would be applicable (a) when the inclusion of costs like material and subcontracting would distort the allocation of G&A expense in relation to benefits received and (b) when costs other than direct labor are significant measures of total activity; and (3) single-element cost input (direct labor hours or direct labor dollars, for example), which would be applied when their use will produce equitable results. CAS 410 also provides that a special allocation be made by deducting from the G&A expense pool and base (input costs) those costs applicable to subcontracting, material, and other costs when subcontracting, material, and other costs are significant and will not receive the full benefit of G&A expense if one of the three methods described above is used.

Most of the flexibility in the treatment of costs disappeared when the Cost Accounting Standards Board was established and standards prompted by contractors' irregular and improper accounting of costs were promulgated. Today, the distortion of costs and the sizable amount of added cost to the government in its purchase of supplies and services can be attributed to DCAA's treatment of costs, its interpretation and implementation of contract costs principles, and the Cost Accounting Standards. And that distortion is aggravated by the significant increase of G&A costs since the 1950s, an increase that is due partly to the additional reporting requirements imposed on contractors by the government. Most costly has been DCAA's handling of costs under CAS 403 and CAS 410. The net result has been added profits for major contractors in the form of G&A, because indirect rates are computed by dividing the expense pool (anticipated or actual) by the base total cost input (anticipated or actual). Many major contractors have elected not to have a special allocation for the handling of materials, subcontracting, and other costs for which the only services the contractor performs are negotiating and signing a contract, receiving the merchandise, and paying the bills. When hundreds of millions of dollars in subcontracting are involved, use of the full G&A rate based on total cost input results in a lower G&A rate, although the contractor's allocation of G&A expense for its in-house efforts (direct labor, overhead, etc.) might result in underrecovery, whereas administrative costs for handling purchases of material and subcontracting are grossly overrecovered. Stated another way: Both administrative costs for work performed in house and administrative costs associated with subcontracts are improperly stated.

Suppose, for example, the cost of subcontracting is $20 million and the contractor adds 20%, ($4 million), for G&A expense, and another 10% for total costs ($2.4 million), for profit making the selling price $26.4 million. For its services of negotiating and signing a $20 million subcontract, receiving the goods and services, and receiving and paying invoices, the prime contractor receives $4 million for administrative costs and $2.4 million in profit.

Such machinations are buried in the contractor's annual reports to stockholders, because cost elements as presented are completely different and because income, costs, and profits for government and nongovernment business are combined. G&A income has nothing to do with the establishment of the G&A rate, nor does the government routinely keep tabs on G&A income.

A major contractor could take a financial beating if, after establishing and quoting rates based on a high percentage of subcontracting, a major portion of its new business involved few costs that would be subject to a special allocation. If that situation occurred, however, the firm's G&A rate would have to increase: Because most major contracts are fixed-price-incentive contracts and at any point contain numerous changes and unpriced actions, ample room exists to recover costs.

G&A expense in the 1950s usually did not include costs of IR&D or B&P or other direct costs; the rate was based on cost of goods sold, a considerably smaller base; and subcontracting was minimal. Today, DCAA generally insists on the use of the total cost input base, even though its use will result in the distortion of expenses allocated to government contracts when a significant volume of subcontracting and materials purchased is involved. G&A expense for major government contractors is now approximately seven times greater than it was in the 1950s, when expenses for IR&D and B&P were included in overhead, subcontracting was considerably less, and G&A was allocated on a considerably smaller base.

IR&D/B&P. In the 1950s, IR&D and B&P for major firms were generally included in overhead and amounted to approximately 15% of direct labor dollars, the base for allocating overhead. Today, both are included in G&A, and combined, are approximately 4–10% of total cost input, a base much greater than the direct labor base that includes subcontracting, which for major system prime contractors amounts to approximately 50% of sales. Accordingly, IR&D and B&P have increased substantially since the 1950s.

The government recognizes these as essential costs and permits contractors to charge IR&D and B&P expenses up to a specified amount against government business. According to the Federal Acquisition Regulation (FAR), the contract cost principles, and the Cost Accounting Standards, major government contractors, to be reimbursed for IR&D and B&P expense, must have received a total of over $4.4 million for those costs in the prior fiscal year and must sign an advance agreement with the government for the current year or be subject to a fine. Under the guidelines, major contractors must submit a proposal to the government citing anticipated projects and the expenses for each and agreeing that any amount over a cited ceiling will be borne by the contractor. Indications are, however, that the government has no established method or procedure for monitoring claims for IR&D and B&P.

IR&D. For the contractor to be reimbursed, according to the FAR, projects need not be directly related to the government's needs, nor need they be truly related to R&D. Many firms benefit from the government's requirements for research and development as these requirements relate to the firms' commercial products. At the same time, firms that undertake R&D at their own expense in an effort to corner the government market are taking a large risk because no one can ensure that they will be awarded a contract based on the research. Procurement regulations emphasize the need for competition, which is assured by the government's preference for preparing its own specifications or work statements; but when the government prepares its requirements, a firm that has already performed the research may be left out in the cold or forced to divulge its secrets. Thus, the government's attempt to have industry absorb more system development costs runs counter to the realities of the situation.

Historically, major firms have spent approximately 2% of sales for costs of R&D and reported them under overhead expense or separately as research and development. Today, that amount ranges from 1-5% of total cost input (not sales) for major government contractors and is generally included under G&A. If subcontracted costs are excluded from the base, the range would be approximately 2-10%. In billing, IR&D is usually included in G&A. Furthermore, in accordance with the Cost Accounting Standards, this cost is excluded from bearing its share of G&A expense, because the CASB contends that IR&D includes the G&A, administrative, and management expense of an entire business unit. It does not. The result is that other projects must be charged a higher rate for overhead to make up the deficit.

B&P. Today the cost of preparing bids and proposals is included in G&A expense, but in the 1950s it was generally included in overhead because technical personnel were involved. Accordingly, the base for the allocation of B&P expense has changed drastically. Today, it represents approximately 4–8% of *total cost input,* a much greater base than *direct labor dollars,* used for the allocation of overhead in the 1950s, when it represented approximately 5% of direct labor dollars. Accordingly, B&P has increased significantly since the 1950s.

An Additional Comment

Table 3 (see chapter 2) shows that if overhead, G&A expense, costs of IR&D and B&P, and profit on subcontracts were treated today the way they were in 1950, the saving in formal contract expenditures would be approximately 53%—$71 billion. Table 3 also shows that G&A expense has increased approximately 1000%, and fringe benefits approximately 400%. What the table does not highlight is that overhead has also increased, despite the fact that costs of IR&D and B&P have been extracted and made part of G&A expense, resulting in an additional benefit to the contractor, as costs of IR&D and B&P do not share in the allocation of the firm's G&A expense.

Having become accustomed to receiving full profit on subcontracted costs, major government contractors will likely resist any efforts to remove these bonanzas. Furthermore, the overrecovery of G&A, IR&D, and B&P expenses is more likely to ensure a firm's profitability than is profit.

The picture of costs is even bleaker when second-, third-, and fourth-tier subcontracts are considered. A $10 part purchased by a fourth-tier subcontractor and passed on to the third-, second-, and first-tier subcontractors, each adding 20% for G&A expense and 10% for profit, would result in the prime contractor's paying $83.96 ($63.61 for purchased part, $12.72 for G&A expense, and $7.63 for profit). The prime contractor's charge to the government would be $124.02 ($93.96 for the purchased part, $18.79 for G&A expense, and $11.27 for profit). Had any labor and overhead been included along the way, costs would have increased significantly.

Accordingly, DOD's recent trend toward awarding contracts for major systems to joint ventures appears to be a step in the wrong direction, adding as it does another layer of costs and profits. Although the work would be divided between the partners in the joint venture, possibly eliminating the peaks and valleys in the aerospace industry, a legal monster has been created. Using R&D and financial risks as reasons for encouraging joint ventures appears to run counter to historical considerations. First, statutes permit the government to aid financially any firm for national security reasons. Second, the government is reimbursing major government contractors approximately $18 billion a year for IR&D costs—an amount over and above what the government has already budgeted for R&D contracts.

A recent regulation from DOD prohibits the inclusion of G&A expense in the factors for determining profit, decreases the weighting factor on labor, and places more emphasis on capital employed. The resulting profit rate for small firms and strictly R&D firms is reduced approximately 40% whereas the profit rate for the government's major contractors is reduced approximately 9%. Those guidelines are not in accordance with generally accepted business or accounting practices and do not attack the illness in the procurement process—which is that G&A expense is the mainstay for most major government contractors. It attacks the symptoms—and the loser, small businesses and strictly R&D firms whether small, medium or large.

The government's procurement process should not be used as a means of subsidizing a company's commercial endeavors. Present policies have resulted only in management's looking to the government for handouts.

5.
Profit

Profit is the amount left after all expenses are deducted. In financial circles, profit is viewed from many perspectives, the most common being sales and return on investment. For investors and financial institutions, profit is a major concern because of potential dividends and the effect on the price of a company's stock. Any corporation with sales in the hundreds of millions of dollars and a profit rate of 4–5% is doing extremely well.

In the commercial sector, many products and services are sold at a loss. When contractors sell their products to related foreign sales corporations at cost or below and up to 15% of the foreign sales corporation's profits are exempted from federal income tax, sales to the foreign corporation will adversely affect the domestic firm's overall profitability. In other instances, profitability is contingent on a firm's ability to exceed an anticipated sales volume. Thus, government contractors' profit on nongovernment sales is at best distorted and in many cases questionable. Rarely is it based on a rigid pricing formula, as required by the government Cost Accounting Standards or cost principles.

Consider, for example, the development of a new military aircraft with potential sales to allied countries. The government pays for the development—usually worth billions of dollars—and the production of 100 planes. The contractor's subsequent sales of the planes should be extremely profitable to the contractors involved: No procedure exists for prorating the cost of the design, development, and tooling over any more than the first 100 planes. Contractors should be required, however, to base the cost to the government on the anticipated number of planes to be sold, just as they do in the private sector. If the firm sells more than the anticipated number, it will do well financially; if it sells fewer than the estimated number, it will lose money.

In the 1950s, when significant amounts of subcontracting and purchase of materials were involved in the performance of a contract, procurement personnel would determine the administrative and managerial effort and expense involved and would assess a rate for service or materials handling commensurate with the anticipated administrative cost plus a considerably reduced profit on those costs. In the 1980s, however, although subcontracting has increased from approximately 30% in the 1950s to approximately 50–70% of the selling price and the procurement budget has increased severalfold, major government contractors receive the full profit, or approximately 12%, on those costs—which equals just below 11% of sales. On a $2 billion program, for example, $1 billion might be subcontracted, divided into $893 million in costs and $107 million profit. For acting as the middle man on the subcontract, the prime contractor will be able to charge the government its normal profit for the contract—say 12%, or $120 million—which is more than the subcontractor earns, having supplied the material, labor, and production resources and having assumed the risk for its performance on the program. In terms of profit received in relation to in-house contribution (labor, overhead, G&A, etc.), the profit (assuming costs and profit are the same as the subcontracted effort) would be $214 million (24%) on $893 million in costs. And this calculation does not take into consideration the additional profit to be made by the prime contractor in the form of G&A, materials handling, and service charges.

Another matter concerns the base for determining profit. The profit rate cited by government procurement personnel and by a company for specification items used in the commercial field invariably means profit as a percentage of *cost*. Articles and books on financial matters, however, invariably refer to profit as a percentage of *sales*. The Renegotiation Board, now defunct, whose function was to recover excessive profits from government contractors, also looked at profit as a percentage of sales. Thus, contractors that filed with the Renegotiation Board were automatically granted a 1% additional profit as a starting point, since 10% (profit) of costs equals just below 9% of sales. The Vinson-Trammel Act imposed a limit on profits for the shipbuilding industry, but in 1981 Congress put the act in limbo, to be reactivated only in an emergency.

No matter what the basis for profit and whether or not earned, once it is received, labor generally asks for a wage increase and/or added fringe benefits. The result is an upward spiral of costs. Although profit should reflect a company's overall performance, risk, and return on investment, the fact remains that profits of the major government contractors do not reflect any of those elements.

Major government contractors' technical performance and ability to meet a contract's requirements for cost and delivery schedule are matters of record. They are atrocious. The government is not entirely blameless, however. Contracts and procurement specifications for major systems are generally so ambiguous and contradictory that contractors are ensured reimbursement. And many contractors who fail the first time around on a technical requirement are given contract modifications with new money—to try again. But even if the contract and specifications were perfect, the government could, by statute for national security reasons, financially bail out a contractor. The bulk of the contractual claims against the government have been attributed to intangible losses—lost time, lost efficiency, lost income—rather than to constructive or engineering changes. Accordingly, while the technological requirements sought by the government are continually more stringent, major government contractors have fared very well. Problems can often be traced to poor management and the failure of a commercial endeavor, nevertheless major contractors invariably receive most of the aid requested.

With regard to return on investment, the government, in addition to making progress payments amounting to billions of dollars, furnishes plants and equipment to its contractors, which might also be worth billions of dollars. When the plant and equipment amount to a government-owned/company-operated facility, the profit, based on costs, should be approximately 0.5%, rather than 10–12% of costs. Major government contractors are grossly undercapitalized once progress payments, fast write-off of assets, government-furnished plant, equipment, and facilities, and contractor-acquired government property are deducted.

The treatment of profit for government contracts involving major systems has been too lax and slanted in the wrong direction. The result is excessive profits and an ever-spiraling increase in costs to offset the excesses, and it comes from the weighting factors used for the various costs and risk, the "Weighted Guidelines Profit/Fee Objective." DOD's recent change in the weighting factors for determining the profit rate seriously downgrades the significance of the labor force to be used and puts menial labor on practically the same level as the most sophisticated scientific labor—a factor that can only discourage small research firms (the firms that have made the most significant scientific contributions and that employ the largest number of truly research-oriented personnel) from doing business with the government. The new guideline is directed solely at granting major government contractors an inflated profit rate by relying heavily on the dollar amount of capital employed, which historically has been overstated. Accordingly, the weighted guidelines method of determining profit and fees should be rescinded.

Government contractors are entitled to a reasonable profit, but that profit should *not* be based on the weighted guidelines method of determining profit and fees when the type of contract (risk), capital employed, and performance are the major weighting factors. The problem with such a quantified approach is that it must be everything to everyone and is therefore meaningless. And although the new regulation that excludes G&A in the computation of profit might not be damaging to major contractors, it is devastating to small, research-oriented companies.

It appears that the nation, thanks to the government, has lost its sense of values. Either that or the government (DOD and Congress, the forces behind the weighted guidelines method of determining profit) definitely wants to force small companies out of the government marketplace.

Some questions are appropriate to ask when reviewing profits reported by major government contractors:

1. How much was invested in acquiring an interest in or purchasing outright other firms that might have experienced losses and therefore reduced their true profitability or return on investment?

2. How much are the contractors paying in bonuses (stock, cash, etc.)?

3. How much did it cost the government to enable its major system contractors to perform tasks that could have been performed more economically by other firms?

4. How much of a firm's government procurement income is expended for its nongovernment business?

5. How much of its costs are unallowable (according to government regulations)?

6. How much were its sales to its foreign sales corporation?

7. What is the value of GFP?

8. What is the value of GFE?

9. What is the current amount of unliquidated progress payments?

10. What is the current annual charge for depreciation?

11. What is the value of subcontracting and the percentage of sales on its government business?

6.
The Procurement Process and Staffing

Procurement staff are usually subordinate to an agency's comptroller, project office, or administrative office —none of which generally has any knowledge of government procurement regulations, statutes, procedures, and practices. These offices are concerned primarily that the monies appropriated be spent in the fiscal year they are appropriated, not with how the monies are spent or whether the spending complies with applicable regulations.

Suppose, for example, a $3 million contract is negotiated during the tenth month of the fiscal year, and the buyer negotiates a $500,000 reduction in price. If the money had been specified for a particular use, the agency loses the money and the $500,000 is returned to the Treasury. Congress subsequently reduces the agency's request for funds by a corresponding amount in the following fiscal year. The buyer, rather than being a hero, is a troublemaker who took two to three months too long to negotiate the contract, causing the agency to be regarded askance by Congress. In other words, a government buyer is recognized more for his or her knowledge of internal procedures and channels of approval than for business acumen about contractual terms, conditions, cost analysis, and negotiation.

A number of shortcuts had been instituted to facilitate

the award of contracts—shortcuts such as citing an unrealistic time to respond to the solicitation, foregoing a preaward audit, foregoing cost analyses and negotiations. The Competition in Contracting Act of 1984 (P.L. 98-369) specifies a fixed period for publicizing and responding to a solicitation, thereby eliminating one shortcut. In so doing, however, it has given many small companies the false belief that they have a chance to be awarded those contracts. The bill pending before Congress to eliminate preaward audits under certain conditions underscores the major discrepancy in the procurement process: Congress, the agencies, and supervisors of procurement personnel dictate the course to be followed without relieving the contract buyers of their responsibility concerning the reasonableness of the price. And when the buyers request audits to satisfy concerns about the prices of contracts, they are not likely to win points from their supervisors.

If procurement is to proceed in the allotted time, the shortcuts are a necessity. The shortcuts, however, only add to the morass. Intensifying the problem are inadequately trained staff and poorly staffed and equipped offices.

Under the present organizational structure, each agency and/or administration requires different qualifications for its procurement personnel. And they are frequently placed in an area that does not take advantage of their knowledge and skills.

Funding to train personnel has always been a low priority, and training has been sporadic rather than continual. Even though many agencies have adopted a career advancement curriculum for government procurement personnel, many of the curriculum's goals are unrealistic and unattainable. The number of courses available does not satisfy the curriculum, and many courses have no relationship to the workplace.

Many procurement offices have no cost analysts; others

are grossly understaffed in cost analysts. If costs are to be contained, however, this position is vital.

Procurement offices are also often understaffed in terms of clerical personnel. Thus, buyers must perform many clerical tasks, detracting from their main function.

Many agencies have no lawyers with experience in government contract law. Consequently, buyers themselves must assemble solicitations and contracts, again detracting from their main function. Further, contract clauses, regulations, and practices are ambiguous, contradictory, and confusing. Their interpretation and application vary from agency to agency and within agencies, and the entire area needs review, clarification, and standardization.

Many procurement offices have no word processors or microcomputers, worsening the already poor allocation of human resources. The result is a maze of incompatible instructions, practices, and reporting formats—and needless duplication of effort.

7.
The Renegotiation Board and the Vinson-Trammel Act

Despite the fact that the Renegotiation Board operated for 30 years, few people knew its purpose or its criteria for evaluation. The board's original mandate was to recapture excessive profits, and the regulations it established for the most part gave industry more than the benefit of the doubt. Considering its annual appropriation and staffing levels, however, the board's dollar returns far exceeded those of any other review group.

Congress dealt the Renegotiation Board a serious blow when, in 1971, it changed industry's channel for appeal from the tax court to the court of claims. Three major factors were involved: (1) Personnel from the court of claims did not possess the expertise of those from the tax court in matters of accounting and taxes, which formed the basis for refunds; (2) the burden of supporting its position was transferred from industry to the government; and (3) proceedings before the court of claims were more costly and more drawn out.

In the space of two years, Congress eliminated all vestiges of government review of government contractors' profits. In 1979, the House Appropriations Committee terminated the Renegotiation Board by refusing to approve an annual appropriation for it. The move was very unusual, since the prerogative of terminating a government activity usually rests with the congressional committee that sponsors enabling legislation, not with the Appropriations Committee. Accordingly, the Senate committee members were spared having to go on record for killing the board. The second blow occurred in FY 1981, when Congress set aside the Vinson-Trammel Act (governing profits to be retained by shipbuilders and related industrial firms), stipulating that it be reactivated only in an emergency.

The board's critics claimed that the money returned to the government through the board's actions was minimal, refusing to recognize that the board's original mandate was to act merely as a "governor" on profits earned by government contractors. Congress continually discouraged and rejected efforts by the board to tighten the original mandate.

Several points about the Renegotiation process are noteworthy; as follows:

1. Contractors having aggregate sales of $1 million or more to a limited number of agencies, either as a prime contractor or as a subcontractor, had to file annually with the board. A firm making an identical item for a covered agency and an uncovered agency would find a significant part of its sales to the government not covered by the act.

2. The board's determinations were based on a contractor's annual profit on its overall government (renegotiable) sales, not on the profit contract by contract or item by item.

3. The board's decisions about refunds constituted repricing and resulted in amended state and federal income tax returns. Accordingly, the refund was offset by a tax credit, which in some cases cancelled out the refund.

4. Profits for companies that filed with the board were considered a percentage of sales rather than a percentage of cost, (the latter was the basis for preparing quotations for the government). Accordingly, contractors that were reviewed

were granted an extra percentage point of profit, since 10% of cost equals 8.9% of sales.

5. Firms in industries that historically reported profits of 4 or 5% would be granted profits of at least 10% of sales before a refund was considered.

6. One of the board's unwritten policies was to forego any attempt to recover excessive profits on government business if the contractor reported a loss on its federal income tax return.

7. By statute, the Renegotiation Board was the only group within the government that had access to all of the contractor's financial information.

8. Government contractors were not required to report costs for government business, in accordance with established government contract costing principles and practices.

9. Government contractors were permitted to file income, costs, and expenses using a sales ratio for the allocation of costs for commercial and government business—thereby offsetting the profitability of government business—unless it was known that a specific contract lost money. In that case, actual costs were used as the basis for the treatment of costs.

10. In general, the board's policy regarding profit was to allow a contractor at least the same profit on its government business that it earned on its nongovernment business.

11. The board did not attempt to isolate the capital investment actually used in the performance of government contracts, compared with that used in nongovernment contracts.

12. Renegotiation was based on a firm's federal income tax return to determine overall income, expenses, and profit.

13. Most major government contractors with significant claims against the government did not report the claims in their federal income tax returns or to their stockholders.

Thus, the amount of the claim in practically all cases went unreported and therefore unscrutinized by the board.

14. The board made no attempt to determine the dollar value of GFE, GFP, or contractor-acquired property used in performing government contracts.

15. The board made no attempt to determine the value of the government property that major government contractors used in performing nongovernment contracts.

16. The board gave no attention to sales a major government contractor made to its domestic international sales corporation (now called foreign sales corporation). The statute authorizing the sales corporation precluded its inclusion on a firm's consolidated federal income tax return.

17. Although the board had the authority to disallow some salaries, the process of disallowing them was time consuming and seldom used.

8.
Conclusions and Recommendations

The United States needs—indeed, should have—the best defense capability in the world, whatever the cost. A major obstacle to satisfying that need, however, is the government's acquisition process, both its organization and its policies. The government's adoption of the concept of systems procurement in the late 1950s contributed significantly to increased costs for all major systems because of the necessity for increased subcontracting. The introduction of four or more commands in the procurement process—the user, the procuring organization, the audit group (DCAA), and the contract administration group (DLA)—further complicated the process and increased the costs. DCAA and DLA have detracted from the contract specialists' responsibilities and authority, raising a serious question about who is responsible for negotiating the price of a contract—the buyer, the auditor, the field administrative contracting officer, the project manager, the agency or department head, or the inspector general. Although procurement regulations state that the contracting officer alone is responsible for ascertaining the reasonableness of a price, numerous statutes and contract terms make that designation questionable. P.L. 96-304, for example, the Supplemental Appropriations and Rescission Act of 1980, requires audits to be resolved within six months after the final audit report is issued. P.L. 97-255, the Federal Management Financial Integrity Act of 1982, resulted in the Comptroller General's issuing standards for internal controls in the federal government in 1983. These statutes and internal regulations give the auditors and other personnel more responsibility than the buyer in resolving contested costs. Furthermore, the time stipulated is unrealistic and is to industry's benefit.

When a single subcontractor supplies the parts and the prime contractor has only to install the item, the item costs the government 30% more than if purchased direct from the manufacturer—plus G&A expense and profit of more than twice that charged by the manufacturer. When additional layers of subcontracting are added, the costs increase even more. Innovative research, historically performed by small businesses, has been crushed or at best discouraged, as approximately 90% of the government's procurement dollars (mostly in the form of system contracts that involve R&D, system design, fabrication, maintenance, and repair) are awarded to a handful of contractors. Today, approximately 4% of the government's procurement monies are awarded to small businesses, which for the most part compete against one another and result in numerous business failures.

The government could secure considerably more for its appropriated funds by changing the procurement process. It could also save money by improving its in-house technical capability, especially in the preparation of procurement specifications and the evaluation of contractor technical and cost proposals. And, again, the concept of systems procurement is at fault. Overall, the procurement process is burdened with meaningless coordination and channels of approval and encumbered with unduly restrictive legislation and accounting, legal, and business guidelines.

Several major changes should be made in the areas of

procurement function and organization, policy, costing/ auditing, and negotiation. These changes follow...

- *Procurement function and organization*

1. Establish a separate federal procurement agency with complete authority and responsibility in all phases of procurement, including the establishing and implementing of all policies, procedures, and practices.

The establishment of a separate procurement agency has several advantages:

A. The use of uniform procurement regulations, practices, and policies within agencies and between agencies.

B. A restriction on the role of the user during negotiation so prices can be negotiated on the basis of supportive cost data.

C. The establishment and enforcement of checks and balances, to result in more—clearly—defined work statements and specifications.

D. The removal of negotiation from the project (technical) side.

E. The establishment of uniform work standards or procurement standards for procurement personnel, based on specific performance criteria.

F. The assurance that staffing of procurement offices will be based on realistic criteria uniformly applied.

G. The establishment of a training division within the agency to coordinate and develop procurement training programs for the entire government procurement force.

H. The assurance that GFP, GFE, and contractor-acquired property will be properly accounted for and covered contractually.

I. More accurate and timely reporting of budgeted, committed, obligated, and paid out funds.

J. The establishment of a division for automatic data processing to coordinate, define, budget, and implement office automation for individual procurment offices.

K. The establishment of uniform software for all procurement needs.

L. Uniformity of solicitations, contracts, and costing requirements.

M. More accurate reporting of government procurement activity.

N. Earlier detection of technical and financial problems on major programs.

2. Establish a new senior procurement job classification with the title Procurement Planning/Coordination Specialist, whose function would be to coordinate requirements with agency personnel from the time an item is introduced into the agency's budget.

3. Review the overall procurement process for ways to shorten it.

4. Abolish DCAA, rescind its manual, and transfer its functions to the new procurement agency.

5. Abolish DLA's procurement activities and transfer them to the procurement agency.

6. Eliminate the Office of Federal Procurement Policy (OFPP) within the Office of Management and Budget and transfer its functions to the procurement agency.

7. Improve the government's in-house technical capability for the preparation of specifications/statements of work and evaluation of technical proposals.

8. Establish one committee in the Senate and one in the House to promulgate all legislation affecting procurement.

9. Restrict the issuance of updates to regulations to two or three times a year.

10. Review all statutes, regulations, and clauses to eliminate ambiguities, overcome judicial decisions that run counter to the intent of the contract and the interests of the nation and its taxpayers, and ensure that the buyer has com-

plete and undivided responsibility and authority in the procurement process.

11. Establish severe penalties for government personnel who ignore procurement statutes and regulations.

- *Policy*

1. Require the agencies to modify the system procurement concept and procure major subsystems directly and furnish them to the prime contractor as GFE.

2. Give the government more authority in "make-or-buy" decisions.

3. Require the agencies to abandon the self-governance policy.

4. Prohibit the use of price analysis in all negotiated contracts and make cost analysis mandatory.

5. Legally restrict the use of fixed-price incentive contracts to follow-on production contracts.

- *Costing/auditing*

Simplify and clarify costing for government contracts by

1. Requiring contractors to submit copies of their latest financial statements to the contracting officer with their cost proposals.

2. Requiring a detailed cost proposal on all negotiated procurements.

3. Following generally accepted accounting practices, which should be reflected in the FAR.

4. Rescinding the Cost Accounting Standards, either transferring them to Part 31 of the FAR or deleting them.

5. Requiring detailed cost schedules in support of all indirect cost pools.

6. Restricting contractors to a maximum of four cost centers—services, manufacturing, R&D, and construction.

7. Expanding Part 31 of the FAR to define the

categories of cost to be treated as direct and indirect in each of the four cost centers proposed, and to reflect the treatment and reporting requirements for the base and expense pool for all indirect cost rates.

8. Requiring contractors to certify that the treatment of costs (direct/indirect) for government contract business is the same as that accorded costs on their nongovernment business.

9. Discontinuing the differential treatment and audit requirements of costs for firm-fixed-price contracts and cost-reimbursement contracts.

10. Rescinding the treatment accorded IR&D and B&P costs as provided for in the Cost Accounting Standards and the FAR and requiring that they be included in overhead and assume their share of G&A expense.

11. Disallowing bonuses as a cost of doing business with the government.

12. Establishing formal guidelines for the treatment of fringe benefits and require that it be treated as a separate cost category to be included as part of labor costs (direct/indirect), as applicable, thereby affecting the computation of indirect rates.

13. Establishing formal guidelines for material handling costs.

14. Legislating a ceiling on the percentage of labor costs that can be charged for fringe benefits.

- *Negotiation*

1. Pass a statute providing that a contractor's failure to submit requested detailed cost information and financial statements in time for negotiations would be grounds for declaring the contractor nonresponsive (for new contracts) or in default (for contract modifications), with the profit rate automatically reduced to 50% of the

anticipated profit rate for the task or effort involved.

2. Limit by law the amount of add-on costs charged for overhead, G&A expense, service charges, and profit on subcontracts and purchases of materials and spare parts by major system contractors.

3. Rescind the weighted guidelines method for determining profit.

4. Permit interest expense as an allowable cost on the dollar amount of the contract costs not reimbursed by progress payments.

5. For proposals estimated to cost over a specified dollar amount to prepare, require the government to restrict the solicitation to a specified number of offerors known to have the capabilities and desire to quote and award a firm-fixed-price, Bid and Proposal contract to each. When commercial-type equipment and/or services are involved, B&P contracts should be prohibited.

6. Discontinue the practice of penalizing agencies that do not expend all appropriated funds by returning the unused monies to the Treasury or reducing future appropriations requests.

These recommendations will simplify the procurement process, define the responsibility and authority of the various groups involved, eliminate multiple commands in the process, and clarify requirements for accounting and auditing—all of which could immediately reduce the government's expenditures for procurement by $15 billion to $25 billion annually. Other savings that would be realized would bring the total saved to approximately $50 billion annually. These changes would assist in improving our industrial base, encourage R&D (especially among small businesses), and give the nation the defense capabilities it needs.

Glossary

Contract close out. Resolution of GFP, patents, claims, and so on before a contract can be closed.

Contractor-acquired property. Facilities and/or equipment purchased by a contractor, using contract funds.

Cost accounting practice. Any disclosed or established accounting method or technique used for measurement of cost, assignment of cost to cost accounting periods, or allocation of cost to cost objectives.

(a) *Measurement of cost* encompasses accounting methods and techniques used in defining the components of cost, determining the basis for cost measurement, and establishing criteria for use of alternative cost measurement techniques. The determination of the amount paid or a change in the amount paid for a unit of goods and services is not a cost accounting practice. Examples of cost accounting practices involving measurement of costs include (i) the use of either historical cost, market value, or present value; (ii) the use of standard cost or actual cost; or (iii) the designation of those items of cost that must be included in or excluded from tangible capital assets or pension cost.

(b) *Assignment of cost to cost accounting periods* refers to a method or technique used in determining the amount of cost to be assigned to individual cost accounting periods. Examples of cost accounting practices involving the assignment of cost to cost accounting periods are requirements for the use of specified accrual basis accounting or cash basis accounting for a cost element.

(c) *Allocation of cost to cost objectives* includes both direct and indirect allocation of cost. Examples of cost accounting practices involving allocation of cost to cost objectives are the accounting methods or techniques used to accumulate cost, to determine whether a cost is to be directly or indirectly allocated, to determine the composition of cost pools, and to determine the selection and composition of the appropriate allocation base.

Cost Accounting Standard. Promulgations by the CASB citing accounting principle(s), practices, or criteria to be applied by major government contractors in selecting from various alternatives in estimating, accumulating, and reporting costs of contracts.

Cost analysis. An analysis of costs as shown in the cost breakdown submitted in support of a contractor's price.

Cost center/segment. One of two or more divisions, product department, plants, or other subdivisions of an organization reporting directly to a home office, usually identified with responsibility for profit and/or producing a product or service. The term includes government-owned/contractor-operated facilities and joint ventures and subsidiaries (domestic and foreign) in which the organization has a majority ownership. The term also includes those joint ventures and subsidiaries (domestic and foreign) in which the organization has less than a majority of ownership but over which it exercises control.

Cost-plus-fixed-fee contract. Cost-reimbursement-type contract that guarantees the contractor actual costs up to the estimated cost cited in the contract plus the cited fixed fee (profit). Used for performance of research when the cost is difficult to ascertain.

Cost-reimbursement contract. A contract that guarantees the contractor actual costs up to the estimated amount cited in the contract; involves no fee (profit).

Also a generic term for contracts that guarantee reimbursement to the contractor of actual costs up to the cited amount in the contract, with or without a fee (profit).

Direct cost. Any cost that is identified specifically with a particular final cost objective. Direct costs are not limited to items incorporated in the end product as material or labor. Costs identified specifically with a contract are direct costs of that contract. All costs identified specifically with other final cost objectives of the contractor are direct costs of those cost objectives.

Firm-fixed-price contract. Contract in which price is not subject to any adjustment by reason of cost experience.

First-in-first-out inventory valuation method. The practice of charging out first, to products or sales, costs of the first received elements of inventory.

107

Fixed-price contract. A generic term given to contracts in which elements of cost have been assigned a fixed price.

Fixed-price incentive contract. Fixed-price-type contract with provision for adjustment of profit and establishment of the final contract price by a formula based on the relationship that the final negotiated total cost bears to total target costs.

Fixed-price redetermination contract (prospective). Fixed-price contract with provision for redetermination of price, either upward or downward, at a stated time during the performance of the contract.

Fixed-price redetermination contract (retroactive). Contract that provides for ceiling price and retroactive price redetermination after completion of the contract.

General and administrative (G&A) expense. Any management, financial, and other expense incurred by or allocated to a business unit that is for the general management and administration of the business unit as a whole. G&A expense does not include those management expenses whose beneficial or casual relationship to cost objectives can be more directly measured by a base other than a cost input base representing the total activity of a business unit during a cost accounting period.

Get well. A situation in which a contractor losing money under a contract is permitted to recoup additional funds through various means, such as engineering charges or changes in location of plant, delivery schedule, and other terms and conditions of the contract.

Horizontally integrated. A firm capable of fabricating one product or service such as fabricating an airframe and assembling all purchased subsystems. In contrast, a vertically integrated firm may fabricate the airframe and numerous subsystems (navaids, armament, instrumentation systems etc.) and assemble all components.

Independent research and development (IR&D) cost. The cost of effort that is neither sponsored by a grant nor required in the perfor-

mance of a contract and that falls within any of the following areas:
(a) basic research,
(b) applied research,
(c) development, and
(d) systems and other concept formulation studies.

Labor-hour contract. Variant of time and material contract, differing in that materials are not supplied by the contractor.

Last-in-first-out inventory valuation method. The practice of charging out first, to products or sales, costs of the last received elements of inventory.

Pools/pooled costs. Costs not readily identifiably to a specific cost objective that are allocable to all business.

Preaward assist audit. An audit performed before award of a contract to verify any number of items, including accounting system, financial condition, productive and engineering resources, labor rates, indirect rates, past performance of contractor, etc.

Price analysis. The comparison of prices between bidders to determine the successful bidder.

Small business. Any concern, firm, person, corporation, partnership, cooperative, or other business enterprise organized pursuant to 15 U.S.C. 637(b)(6) and the rules and regulations of the Small Business Administration set forth in Part 121 of Title 13 of the Code of Federal Regulations. Determined by the industry and the size of a firm relative to other firms in the same industry.

Standard cost. Any cost computed with the use of preestablished measures.

Time and material contract. Procurement of supplies and services on the basis of direct labor hours at specified hourly rates and material at cost.